Ronald J. Sider

FIXING THE MORAL DEFICIT

A Balanced Way to Balance the Budget

IVP Books

An imprint of InterVarsity Press
Downers Grove, Illinois

InterVarsity Press
P.O. Box 1400, Downers Grove, IL 60515-1426
World Wide Web: www.ivpress.com
E-mail: email@ivpress.com

InterVarsity Press® is the book-publishing division of InterVarsity Christian Fellowship/USA®, a
movement of students and faculty active on campus at hundreds of universities, colleges and schools
of nursing in the United States of America, and a member movement of the International Fellowship
of Evangelical Students. For information about local and regional activities, write Public Relations
Dept., InterVarsity Christian Fellowship/USA, 6400 Schroeder Rd., P.O. Box 7895, Madison, WI
53707-7895, or visit the IVCF website at <www.intervarsity.org>.

All Scripture quotations, unless otherwise indicated, are taken from the Holy Bible, New
International Version®. NIV®. Copyright ©1973, 1978, 1984 by International Bible Society.
Used by permission of Zondervan Publishing House. All rights reserved.

Figures 1.2, 2.1, 2.10 and 5.2 are used by permission from the Center on Budget and Policy Priorities
<cbpp.org>. Figures 2.2, 2.4, 2.5, 2.7, 2.8 and 2.9 are used by permission from the Economic Policy
Institute <epi.org>. Table 2.2 is used courtesy of Citizens for Tax Justice <ctj.org>.

Cover design: Cindy Kiple
Interior design: Beth Hagenberg
Image: ©dddb/iStockphoto

ISBN 978-0-8308-3795-3

Printed in the United States of America ∞

Library of Congress Cataloging-in-Publication Data

Sider, Ronald J.
  Fixing the moral deficit: a balanced way to balance the budget /
Ronald J. Sider.
     p. cm.
  Includes bibliographical references (p.   ) and index.
  ISBN 978-0-8308-3795-3 (pbk.: alk. paper)
     1. Economics—Religious aspects—Christianity. 2. Economics—Moral
and ethical aspects. 3. United States—Economic conditions. 4.
United States—Moral conditions. 5. Social justice—Religious
aspects—Christianity. I. Title.
  BR115.E3S475 2012
  261.8'50973—dc23
                                                            2011047329

P   20   19   18   17   16   15   14   13   12   11   10   9   8   7   6   5   4   3   2   1
Y   29   28   27   26   25   24   23   22   21   20   19   18   17   16   15   14   13   12

CONTENTS

ACKNOWLEDGMENTS

This book would have been impossible to write in the short time I had without the superb help in research by Heidi Unruh. Jamison Parker and Amanda Arbour also helped with some research. Gary Cook and Asma Lateef at Bread for the World graciously provided some data.

Bob Greenstein and his colleagues at the Center for Budget and Policy Priorities helped me avoid mistakes and added precision with their careful reading of the manuscript and significant suggestions. Calvin College economist George Monsma did the same as did Jerry Clampet, a colleague at Evangelicals for Social Action.

David Fuller, a Wilberforce Scholar at Palmer Seminary, did a superb job deciphering my handwriting and typing most of the manuscript. My administrative assistant, Joshua Cradic, helped David learn how to read my scribblings and also typed chapter three.

The decision to write this book emerged out of Evangelicals for Social Action's earlier "A Call for Intergenerational Justice: A Christian Proposal on the American Debt Crisis"—a joint project with Stephanie Summers and Gideon Strauss at the Center for Public Justice. ESA colleagues Paul Alexander and

Al Tizon as well as Eastern University graduate student Melissa Yao helped with the Call and ESA's more concrete proposals for implementing it.

Special thanks go to Pauline, Courtney and Howard for allowing me to share their stories and to the Bauman Foundation for a timely grant.

Andy Le Peau courageously agreed to publish the book on a very abbreviated schedule.

Finally, my wife, Arbutus, believed so deeply in this effort that she agreed to excuse me from some of my regular household chores for a couple months. She even allowed me to write one chapter just before we celebrated our fiftieth wedding anniversary.

To all these friends and colleagues, I express my gratitude for their part in making this a better book. For its remaining inadequacies, I accept full responsibility.

ABBREVIATIONS

BFW	Bread for the World
CBO	Congressional Budget Office
CBPP	Center for Budget and Policy Priorities
CRFB	Committee for a Responsible Federal Budget
CRS	Congressional Research Service
Domenici-Rivlin	"Restoring America's Future," November 17, 2010, a report by a bipartisan Debt-Reduction Task Force chaired by former Republican Senator Pete Domenici and Clinton Office of Management and Budget Director Alice Rivlin
GDP	Gross Domestic Product
Simpson-Bowles	Report of the National Commission on Fiscal Responsibility and Reform, December 2010, chaired by former Republican Senator Alan Simpson and former Clinton White House Chief of Staff Erskine Bowles

INTRODUCTION

America faces a historic choice. We have a deficit crisis, a poverty crisis and a justice crisis. And they are all interrelated.

We have a deficit crisis. Do you know which country in the world has the largest debt? The United States. The richest nation in the world is running a huge federal deficit year after year. The national debt is growing at a pace that will eventually produce huge economic problems.

We also have a poverty crisis. Poverty is growing in the richest nation in human history. In the past thirty years the poorest 20% of Americans have become poorer. There are now more Americans living in poverty than at any time in the last fifty years. At the same time, the richest 20% (and especially the richest 5%) have become vastly more wealthy.

Together, the deficit crisis and the poverty crisis produce a justice crisis. Some politicians want to hide their heads in the sand, ignore the debt crisis and keep borrowing. That is flatly immoral. That means putting current expenditures on our grandchildren's credit cards. We want things now but refuse to tax ourselves to pay for them so we simply borrow more money. Our children and grandchildren will have to repay the debt. That is intergenerational injustice.

Other politicians want to balance the federal budget on the

backs of the poor. They propose slashing effective programs that save millions of lives in poor nations and that provide opportunities for and empower poor Americans to escape poverty. At the same time these same politicians want to give more tax cuts to the same wealthy people who have become vastly richer over the last thirty years—even as poor Americans have slipped further into poverty. That is also blatant injustice.

These three crises add up to a huge moral deficit. But there is a balanced way to fix it.

I believe there is a way forward that is both economically wise and morally just. I also believe most American Christians would choose such a path if they understood both the hard economic facts and relevant biblical principles.

This book seeks to provide both. Nobody can be fully objective, but I will try to lay out the facts about how we got into this mess in a way that is as objective and nonpartisan as I can be. I will also spell out the most important biblical principles relative to our situation. Then I will sketch what I believe is a just, workable path out of our triple crisis. There is a balanced way to balance the federal budget.

Make no mistake. The nation faces a momentous choice. How we decide will determine whether America will journey on toward greater liberty and justice for all or descend into gross injustice and dangerous division.

One important note. My writing this book on the specific topic of a just, wise way to solve our budget crisis does not mean I think this is the only important political issue today. I remain committed, as I have for decades, to a biblically balanced political agenda that is pro-life *and* pro-poor, pro-family *and* pro-creation care, pro-sexual integrity *and* pro-peacemaking. The budget crisis is just one of several exceedingly urgent issues today demanding prompt, wise action.

1

THE CRISIS IS REAL

The debt crisis is not some manufactured problem concocted by political fanatics. It is a real, urgent and escalating threat to the future of every American.

Almost every year for more than forty years, the federal government has been running a deficit—that is, spending more money than it takes in that year. The growing national debt (the accumulation of all those years of budget deficits) now puts us on a path where dangerous economic crisis lurks ever closer. Unless we change, our current culture of debt will bankrupt us both economically and morally.

Constantly spending a lot more money than is taken in leads to big economic problems. Virtually all economists agree that continuously allowing the national debt to grow faster than the economy will produce grave economic consequences.

If we continue the current pattern of expenditures and deficits, by 2025 all federal income will be needed simply to pay for social security, Medicare, Medicaid and interest on the national debt. That means the federal government would have to borrow every cent it spent for everything else: education, national defense, homeland security, law enforcement, research, roads—and everything else.[1] Doing that, of course, would produce economic stagnation and a dangerous crisis. And 2025 is only fourteen years away. Simple economics demands that we change.

Figure 1.1 tells the story. Virtually every year since 1960 (except for a few years at the end of President Clinton's presidency and the first year of President Bush's), the federal government has borrowed money because it decided to spend more money than it received in taxes and other fees.

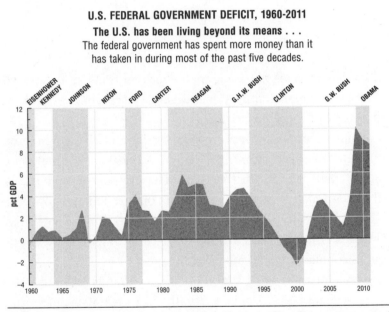

U.S. FEDERAL GOVERNMENT DEFICIT, 1960-2011
The U.S. has been living beyond its means . . .
The federal government has spent more money than it has taken in during most of the past five decades.

Figure 1.1. Source: "A Century of Deficits," compiled by Christopher Chantrill at www.usgovernment debt.us/debt_deficit_history

That is not to say that borrowing money is always a mistake. For individuals and families, it is often wise to borrow to buy a house or car if they have the means to pay back the loan. But we cannot continue year after year spending significantly more than we earn.

The same is true of the federal government.[2] Temporary borrowing is sometimes the wisest policy. The Congressional Research Service is a nonpartisan government-funded center that produces carefully researched reports for all members of Congress. Its October 13, 2011, report titled "The Federal Budget" said: "Most economists agree that, under certain conditions, running a budget deficit may be necessary to provide economic stimulus or pull an economy out of recession. A large budget deficit in a single year, in itself, does not necessarily indicate a longer term problem."[3]

The total amount of taxes falls during a recession. If the federal government temporarily spends borrowed money to get the economy moving again, everyone benefits. That is why—as prominent economists who have won the Nobel Prize for economics point out—a constitutional amendment to require a balanced budget every year is unwise.[4]

Both Presidents George W. Bush and Barack Obama wisely borrowed and spent large sums of money to prevent another Great Depression like that of the 1930s. But it was a fundamental mistake to add substantially to the debt almost every year over the last fifty years. And it will be very dangerous if we keep doing that for the next twenty years.

There are two parts to the federal debt. The larger part is held by the public (individuals, banks, governments and so forth here and around the world). There is also *intragovernmental debt*—that is, money owed by the federal treasury to other governmental entities (e.g., the Social Security Trust Fund). For years, social security taxes brought in more money than was needed for that year's payments, so the federal government "borrowed" the surplus and used it for other current expenditures. Almost all economists agree that the publicly held debt is the problem. That is what affects the economy.

Just how big is the debt? The debt passed $15 trillion in November 2011, with $10.3 trillion of that being publicly held debt.[5] The publicly held debt has more than doubled in the last four years.[6]

The debt crisis seems hard to understand because the numbers involved are so huge. Our government would have had to spend $20 million every day since Jesus was born to reach the size of the present debt. To erase the debt, every man, woman and child in the United States would have to pay $48,000. That is a heavy burden for every baby to start to carry at birth!

U.S. Publicly Held Debt
2009—53% of GDP
2011—75.9% of GDP
2020—90% of GDP (projected)
2035—185% of GDP (projected)

The debt is often stated as a percentage of the country's Gross Domestic Product, which is the sum of all goods and services produced in a given year. In 2009, the publicly held debt was 53% of GDP. President Obama's fiscal year 2011 (FY2011) budget predicted that the publicly held debt would be 75.9% of GDP that year.[7] President Obama's budget for fiscal year (FY) 2011 also projected that the publicly held debt would rise to 90% of GDP by 2020. And the Congressional Research Service said it would go to a disastrous 185% of GDP by 2035.[8]

Economists agree that a national debt nearing the size of the country's annual GDP produces dangerous economic consequences. It means that huge amounts of each year's income from taxes must be devoted to paying the interest on the debt rather than educating our youth, building useful infrastructure and doing research to create a more successful future economy. In addition, people buying or holding the debt begin to worry that the government might not be able to repay the debt, so they invest their money elsewhere and drive up the interest rate paid on the debt. As a result the economy loses steam, people lose jobs, and everyone suffers.

One disturbing aspect of the publicly held debt is that the United States owed (as of December 2010) $1,160,000,000,000 ($1.16 trillion) to mainland China.[9] The fact that the Chinese government owns the largest piece of foreign-held federal debt gives China extra leverage in its dealings with the United States. If Chinese-held U.S. debt continues to grow, that may weaken the United States in its diplomatic, geopolitical interactions with China.

Every year that the federal budget runs a deficit, we add to the debt. Because of the recession, deficits have been especially high in the last three years. The federal deficit was $1.4 trillion for FY2009, $1.3 trillion for FY2010 and $1.3 trillion for FY2011. And unless we change current policies, we will add about one trillion dollars to the federal debt every year for the next ten years.[10]

What are the causes of this explosion of debt? First, as figure 1.2 shows, the economic downturn of the Great Recession of 2007 is the single biggest factor. It caused far lower tax revenues and increased spending on things like food stamps and unemployment insurance. For a couple years, recovery measures (3) and financial bailouts (4) used large amounts of borrowed money, but those factors quickly fade in importance. Almost half of the $20 trillion that the federal government will owe by 2019 results from the wars in Iraq and Afghanistan (1)—they were not paid for with taxes designated for this purpose—and the Bush-era tax cuts (2) of 2001 and 2003.

There is also a long-term factor that is squeezing the federal budget: costs for the three largest programs—social security, Medicare and Medicaid—are increasing faster than the growth of per capita GDP. These expenditures do not require annual action by Congress; they happen automatically unless Congress

ECONOMIC DOWNTURN AND LEGACY OF BUSH POLICIES DRIVE RECORD DEFICITS

Deficit, in trillions

1 ☐ Wars in Iraq and Afghanistan   4 ◼ TARP, Fannie and Freddie
2 ◼ Bush-era tax cuts   5 ◼ Economic downturn
3 ☐ Recovery measures

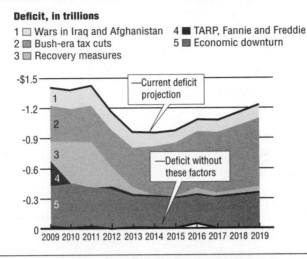

Figure 1.2. Source: CBPP analysis based on Congressional Budget Office estimates. Kathy A. Ruffing and James R. Horney, "Economic Downturn and Bush Policies Continue to Drive Large Projected Deficits," CBPP, May 10, 2011, p. 1.

changes the law. In 2011, federal spending on Medicare and Medicaid was about 5.5% of GDP. But the Congressional Budget Office predicts that those federal health care costs will increase to 10% of GDP by 2035 and 17% by 2080 (primarily because of the aging of the population and the rise in health care costs throughout the entire U.S. health care system). Because of the aging population, the cost of social security will also continue to rise.[11]

Another way to show the rise in mandatory spending is to state the percent of total federal spending devoted to mandatory expenditures. In 1962, mandatory spending took only 25% of the federal budget. By 1975, it took 45%. And in 2009, it was 59.5%.[12]

Policy changes are essential if we want to avoid economic crisis. We need some new mix of increased federal revenues (i.e., more taxes) and reduced federal expenditures. Doing that in a timely, wise fashion will be difficult because the political debate today is more partisan, divisive, nasty and sometimes dishonest than at any time in decades. We will be able to fix our economic—and moral—deficit only if large numbers of citizens demand it.

But we must. Not only to avoid economic disaster but also to promote justice: both intergenerational justice for the future and justice for poor folk now.

Federal Government Mandatory Expenditures
1962—25%
1975—45%
2009—59.5%

It is flatly immoral for my generation of Americans (I am a senior) to demand continuing federal expenditures that we refuse to pay for. Putting my current purchases on my grandchildren's credit cards is outrageous injustice.[13] The Congressional Research Service has estimated that under current policy, "There will be a transfer of resources from future generations to past and present generations of workers equal to $13.6 trillion for social security and $12.5 trillion for Medicare."[14] We must move decisively over the next few years to dramatically reduce and then end ongoing federal budget deficits.

But we dare not do that in a way that neglects poor Americans and poor folk around the world. As we will see in chapter two, poverty continues to grow in the richest nation in history. And many millions of desperately poor people in Africa and elsewhere will simply die unless we continue foreign economic assistance. To try to balance the budget on the backs of the poor would be outrageously immoral.

For twenty years, Roseland Christian Ministries Center on the south side of Chicago ran a program for homeless men. The state helped pay for the program with an annual grant of $380,000. But nine years ago, after the 2001 recession hit, the state slashed its contribution to $190,000, and two years ago the state totally ended its help. In June 2011, Roseland had to shut its doors, ending an effective program for very needy men.[15]

That is not the way to solve governmental budget deficits. The budget crisis is real. We must move decisively to solve it. But it would be immoral to do it, as Amos warned long ago, in ways that "trample on the heads of the poor" (Amos 2:7).

2

CRUCIAL ECONOMIC DATA

"Just the Facts, Ma'am"

To fix the deficit and avoid disaster we need two things. First, a clear understanding of crucial economic facts. And second, a set of relevant biblically grounded moral principles. This chapter outlines the economic data and chapter three presents key principles.

I know that nobody is able to offer a totally objective, totally accurate overview of "the facts." But one can, as I do here, try to use widely accepted sources that most economists and other scholars consider dependable.

The facts on four areas of American economic life will help us understand both the problem and what to do about it: growing poverty, rapidly growing inequality in the distribution of income and wealth, federal taxes, and a comparison of the years 1950-1980 and 1980-2010.

HIGH POVERTY

The richest nation in human history now has the highest poverty level of any Western industrialized nation. And for all but two of the last ten years the poverty level (both the number of people in poverty and the percentage of people in poverty) has grown.

Data from the U.S. Census Bureau (see fig. 2.1) show that for most of the years from 1961 to 2000, the U.S. poverty rate fell. But for the last ten years (except for two years of President George W. Bush's presidency), the poverty rate has increased.[1] The Great Recession (2007) dramatically escalated the number of people in poverty. The latest report (September 2011) from the U.S. Census Bureau reported that in 2010, 46.2 million people (15.1% of all Americans) were in poverty. That was the largest number of people in poverty since the U.S. government started publishing these numbers fifty-two years ago. And it

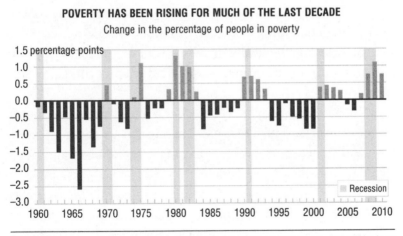

Figure 2.1. Sources: U.S. Census Bureau, National Bureau of Economic Research. www.offthecharts blog.org/today%E2%80%99s-census-report-in-pictures.

was the second highest *rate* in the last forty-five years.[2] As usual, minorities are suffering the most: one in four African Americans and Hispanics were in poverty in 2010, compared to one in ten whites.

The official poverty level in 2010 for a family of four was

$22,314 a year. Some people scoff at the idea that that means poverty.[3] It certainly is not the same as the near absolute poverty that hundreds of millions of people suffer in very poor countries. But households with children living below the poverty level are

- 7 times more likely to experience hunger than households at or above 200% of the poverty line
- 5 times more likely to live in overcrowded housing
- 6 times more likely to be late in paying their rent or mortgage
- more than 3 times more likely to have forgone a visit to the doctor or hospital[4]

I have never met a middle-class Christian raising objections to these statistics who was willing to have his or her family live at or below the poverty level! Furthermore, being in poverty according to the Census Bureau means those people have a total income below the poverty level—often thousands of dollars below. Especially serious is the fact that 20.5 million Americans are in "deep poverty," the Census Bureau reports— that is, they have an annual income of *less than* $11,150 for a family of four (below *half* of the poverty level). Not surprisingly, the number of Americans without health insurance also in- creased to 49.9 million.[5]

The data on poverty I have just cited are from the official poverty reports from the U.S. Census Bureau, using a formula used for decades. But scholars and other experts have long pointed out that the formula is inadequate. It does not count as income important things like food stamps and tax credits that supplement the income of poorer people. Nor does it deduct from income things like taxes and medical expenses. And the formula ignores the fact that it costs much more to live in Man- hattan than in rural Mississippi.

In late 2011 the Census Bureau issued a new report on poverty using a new formula that does take into account the things just mentioned. The new study indicates that the number of Americans in poverty is a little higher—49 million (16%) instead of 46.2 million (15.1%).[6]

One significant thing about the new report is that it helps us see that it is precisely government programs that benefit poor people that help reduce the poverty rate. In 2010, food stamps and tax credits provided $221 billion to poorer people, lifting many millions out of poverty.

More than one out of seven Americans are living in poverty. The number has increased substantially in the last four years. And a crucial reason the number in poverty is not much higher is effective government programs.

SKY-ROCKETING INEQUALITY

Income. The distribution of income in the United States today is more unequal than at any time since 1928, just before the Great Depression. In 2004, the richest 0.1% had more combined pre-tax income than the poorest 120 million.[7] That means if you divided the total U.S. income among one thousand people, the richest person (one person) would have as much income as the poorest 387!

Economists sometimes talk about pre-tax income and after-tax income. Pre-tax income refers to a person's income before he or she has paid taxes, and after-tax income refers to a person's income afterward. Both sets of figures tell the same basic story of enormous and rapidly growing income inequality.

In 2007, the bottom 90% of households—in other words, the vast majority of us—were making, on average, almost $900 less than they made thirty years ago. In contrast, the top 1% of households saw their average pre-tax income increase over that time by $700,000.[8] Another statistic underlines the discrepancy. Census Bureau figures show that the median annual income for a man working full time, year-round in 2010 ($47,715) was *less* in 2010 dollars than in 1973 ($49,065).[9] Over the last three decades the average annual income of the richest 1% has jumped by $700,000 while the average Joe has actually lost ground.

Figure 2.2 shows that from 1979 to 2007, 63.6% of all growth in pre-tax income went to the top 10%—and an astounding 38.7% went to just the top 1%. The bottom 20%, on the other hand, received almost nothing (less than one-half of 1%) of the growth in income. In fact the bottom 90% did not enjoy as much growth in income as the top one percent. That means $1 of every $3 in the growth of pre-tax income in almost thirty years went to the richest 1%. From every $3 of growth, the bottom 20% received less than two cents.

WHERE DID THE GROWTH GO?
Share of pre-tax income growth, 1979-2007

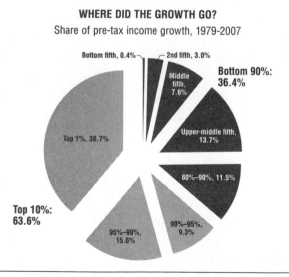

Figure 2.2. Source: EPI analysis of CBO Average Federal Tax Rates and Income, 2010. www.state ofworkingamerica.org/charts/view/82.

The highest gains went to the richest four hundred tax-payers. From 1992 to 2007, each of them increased their pre-tax income 400%. That meant $275 million more per person. But their federal income taxes dropped from a rate of 30% in 1995 to 16.6% in 2007, a tax cut of $46 million per person. Why? Thanks to the cuts in the capital gains tax under President Clinton (1997) and President Bush (2003), the top rate on capital gains and dividends (where the richest make much of their money) is now only 15%—less than half the top tax rate on regular income![10]

The statistics on *after*-tax income tell the same story. According to data from the Congressional Budget Office, in the twenty-eight years from 1979 to 2007, the poorest 20% of Americans experienced a tiny average gain of 16% ($2,400) in *after*-tax income. The middle 20% of Americans did a bit better with a 25% ($11,200) average increase. But the top 20% saw their income jump 95% ($96,600), and the richest 1% enjoyed an astounding increase of 281% ($973,100)![11] On average, the richest 1% were making almost a million dollars more per year in 2007 than in 1979, but the poorest 20% enjoyed, on average, increases of only $2,400.

Even more astonishing, from 1993 to 2007, more than half of all the population-adjusted increase in the nation's income went to the richest 1%. And between 2002 and 2007, two-thirds (two of every three dollars) of increased total U.S. income went to the richest 1%.[12] In 2007 the top 1% had a larger share of total income than at any time since 1928.[13]

Earlier, we saw that the poorest 20% had a tiny bit more income in 2007 than in 1979. But the recession that started that year hit them so hard that by 2009 they were worse off than thirty years earlier. Figure 2.3 shows what happened to the real family income of different groups from 1979 to 2009.

Thanks in part to the Great Recession, the poorest 20% actually had less income (7.4% less) in 2009 than in 1979! But the richest 20% had 49% more and the richest 5% had 72.7% more.[14] Today the United States has a much bigger inequality of income distribution than almost all European countries.[15]

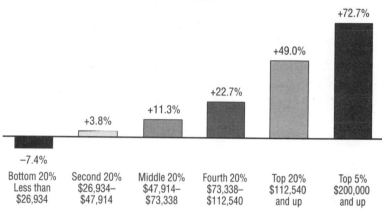

CHANGE IN REAL FAMILY INCOME BY QUINTILE AND TOP 5%, 1979-2009

Figure 2.3. Source: U.S. Census Bureau, Historical Income Tables: Families, Table F-3 (for income changes) and Table F-1 (for income ranges in 2009 dollars). http://inequality.org/income-inequality.

Wealth. The distribution of wealth is even more unequal. Income refers to a person's money received from wages, investments, unemployment benefits, social security and other government cash benefits. Wealth refers to an individual's total accumulated resources (property, stocks, bonds, cars, etc.).

Figure 2.4 shows that in 2009 the bottom 80% of Americans owned just 12.8% of all wealth. The richest 20% owned 87.2%. And the richest 1% alone owned 35.6% of the total wealth in the country—that is more than the total wealth of the bottom 90%! The top 20%, in 2007, owned 91.1% of all stocks.[16]

Figure 2.5 describes the actual wealth of different groups in

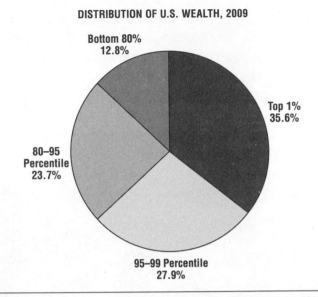

DISTRIBUTION OF U.S. WEALTH, 2009

Bottom 80%
12.8%

Top 1%
35.6%

80–95
Percentile
23.7%

95–99 Percentile
27.9%

Figure 2.4. Source: Economic Policy Institute, The State of Working America 2011, "Wealth Holdings Remain Unequal in Good and Bad Times."http://inequality.org/wealth-inequality.

2009. The poorest 20% have more debts than resources with a negative net worth of minus $27,000. The middle fifth of all Americans have only $65,000 and even the fifth next to the top have only $208,000. But the top 1%, on average, enjoy almost fourteen million dollars ($13,977,000 to be precise).

Furthermore, white Americans on average have a much higher amount of wealth than African Americans and Hispanics. In 2009, the median net worth of white households was $113,145, but for African Americans it was only $5,677 and for Hispanics $6,325.[17] And the gulf between the top and bottom continues to widen. From 1983 to 2004, the bottom 40% of all households saw their net worth drop by 58.7%, but for the richest 20%, it increased almost 80%.[18]

As in the case of income, the distribution of wealth in the United States is far more unequal than in most rich nations.[19]

Furthermore, contrary to the widespread myth of America as the greatest land of opportunity, economic mobility is far lower in the United States than in many European nations. It is far less likely that a poor American will rise from poverty to riches than a poor Canadian, German or French person.[20]

Executive pay. High, escalating executive pay is one reason that the distribution of income and wealth is so unequal. In the late 1960s the average CEO received about twenty-four times

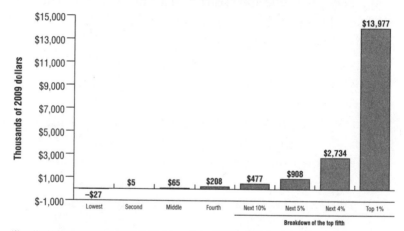

WEALTH SKEWED TOWARDS THE RICHEST OF THE RICH
Average wealth by wealth class in 2009*

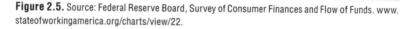

*Note: Wealth is determined by net worth which is assets less liabilities. 2009 data is from Survey of Consumer Finances in 2007 with asset prices to reflect changes from 2007 to 2009 in Flow of Funds data.

Figure 2.5. Source: Federal Reserve Board, Survey of Consumer Finances and Flow of Funds. www.stateofworkingamerica.org/charts/view/22.

as much compensation as the average production worker. In 2009 it was about 185 times as much.[21] In 2010, CEOs at Fortune 500 companies took home 325 times that of the average American worker.[22] That means that each of these Fortune 500 CEOs makes as much in a single day as the average worker makes in about a year and a quarter! And in 2009, the top twenty-five hedge fund managers received total compensation of $25.3 billion—more than $1 billion per person.[23] As in the distribution of income and wealth, the United States is different from continental Europe; American CEOs typically earn 55% more than their European counterparts.[24]

The CEO of Walmart earned as much in one hour in 2008 as many store employees earn in a whole year of full-time work.[25]

Many people don't see anything wrong with these huge increases in executive pay because they see it as the reward for success. If people at the top are taking great risks to make their companies profitable and create jobs for the rest of the country, why shouldn't they be compensated for these efforts?

In fact, executive pay has often come at the expense of, not as a reward for, job creation. For example, at the largest fourteen U.S. financial institutions, between 2000 and 2008, CEOs took home a combined $891 million in cash compensation plus almost $1.8 billion in stock transactions. At the same time, shareholders in these companies received a *negative* 24.8% cumulative return on their investment.[26] CEOs were often rewarded for cutting jobs. In 2009 the fifty CEOs who slashed their payrolls the deepest took home 42% more compensation than the average CEO pay.[27]

Thomas Montag, a leading executive at Bank of America, was awarded a total compensation of almost $30 million ($29,930,431 to be exact) after his company received $45 billion in taxpayer bailouts—and after announcing they were cutting 35,000 jobs. All together, in 2009, five companies that received nearly $131 billion in bailout funds and planned to lay off 110,975 workers gave their highest-paid executives $93,292,406.[28]

We can summarize much of the data on inequality this way: The richest 1% own more of the nation's wealth than the bottom 90%. And the top 1% of tax filers earn much more income each year than the bottom 50% of the population.[29]

Is this fair? Most Americans say no. A solid majority think this huge (and growing) inequality is wrong. Many polls since 1987 by the respected National Opinion Research Center have found that 60% or more of Americans

Richest 1%—more wealth than bottom 90%

Top 1% of tax filers—more income than bottom 50%

agree that "differences in income in America are too large."[30] One national poll from the spring of 2011 discovered that 62% of Americans believed that "one of the biggest problems in this country is that more and more wealth is held by just a few people." Only 24% think this inequality is not a problem.[31]

Dan Ariely does research on behavioral economics. He recently did a study in which he asked Americans how they thought American wealth was distributed. The respondents thought it was distributed significantly more equally than it is.

Then Ariely asked these people to perform a thought experiment: "Imagine that you do not know which wealth group you will be born into. Then imagine that you have the power to decide how the wealth is divided." He then asked the respondents what, under these circumstances, would be the ideal distribution of wealth. Regardless of income, political party or actual wealth, they overwhelmingly favored an "ideal" distribution of wealth that was vastly more equal than what we have today.[32]

Cynthia Carranza runs a food pantry in Illinois. She sees increasingly more needy people coming to her for food while government support is slashed. Cynthia is frustrated because

she knows our rich country could afford to help these hungry
people. She says: "We're an incredibly rich and prosperous
nation. But our wealth is skewed to a very few fortunate at the
top. We're not broke, just twisted."[33]

ARE FEDERAL TAXES HIGH?

Many people think U.S. federal taxes are high. But in reality
American taxes are low by comparison both with most other
developed countries and also with earlier decades in the United
States. Federal taxes have been fairly stable over many decades
as a percent of GDP (although they have hit the lowest level in
decades in the last two years, due to the recession and attempts
to respond). Federal tax rates are actually somewhat lower
today than earlier. Finally, federal taxes are less progressive
now than earlier.

International comparisons. In comparison to almost all
other developed nations, total U.S. taxes are low. Figure 2.6
shows that many rich nations collect 35% to 40%-plus of total
GDP in all taxes. In the United States the percentage is only
26.2% (2008). Almost all the nations in the Organization for
Economic Cooperation and Development (a key organization
of high- and moderate-income nations) have a higher overall
tax take as a percent of GDP.

As percent of GDP. A Congressional Research Service study
has shown that federal taxes have averaged 17.9% of GDP over
more than five decades. Only occasionally did they vary more
than a point or two from that norm.[34] Thanks to the Great Recession, however, current (2011) federal tax receipts are projected to be unusually low at 14.4% of GDP.[35]

Federal taxes are lower today. Both the tax rates and the
percent of income paid in federal taxes are somewhat lower
today than earlier. In 1954 under Republican president Eisen-

TOTAL 2008 TAXES AS A % OF GDP

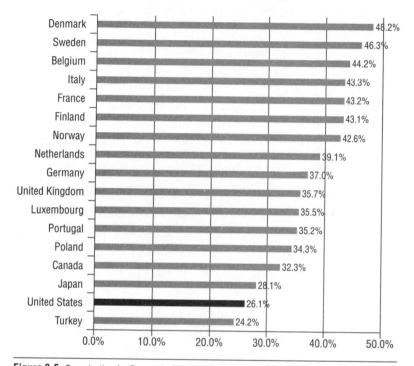

Figure 2.6. Organization for Economic Cooperation and Development (2010), "Total Tax Revenue," Taxation: Key Tables from OECD, no. 2. doi: 10.1787/20758510-2010-table 2. See also Fred Kammer, "U.S. Taxes Are Low by Comparison," *JustSouth Quarterly*, spring 2011, p. 1.

hower, the top income tax bracket was 91%. It dropped to 70% in 1980 and then 28% in 1989. In 1992, under President Clinton, it was increased to 39.6%. Under President Bush, it dropped (in 2003) to 35%, where it is today.

Table 2.1 shows that the percent of income paid in federal taxes has dropped in the last three decades for all income levels. The poorest fifth paid 8% of their total income (including food stamps and other federal assistance) in federal taxes in 1979, but only half that (4%) in 2007. For the top fifth the rate dropped from 27.5% to 25.1%.

AVERAGE FEDERAL TAX RATES PAID BY ALL HOUSEHOLDS,
by Comprehensive Household Income Quintile, 1979-2007

Average tax year	All quintiles	Lowest quintile	Second quintile	Middle quintile	Fourth quintile	Highest quintile	Top 10%	Top 5%	Top 1%
2007	20.4	4.0	10.6	14.3	17.4	25.1	26.7	27.9	29.5
1997	22.9	5.8	13.6	17.4	20.5	28.0	29.9	31.6	34.9
1979	22.2	8.0	14.3	18.6	21.2	27.5	29.6	31.8	37.0

Table 2.1. Source: Congressional Budget Office, June 2010, www.cbo.gov/publications/collections/tax/2010/average_rates.pdf. The tax rates here are based on *comprehensive* income (including nontaxable income like employer-paid health insurance premiums and food stamps), so they are higher than other measures of tax rates.

As figure 2.7 shows, the rich enjoyed the most dramatic tax cuts. The richest 1% paid only 29.5% of their total income in federal taxes in 2007 compared to 37% in 1979. And the top four hundred households did even better as their effective rate dropped from 26.4% (1992) to 16.6%. Tax cuts from 1995 through 2007 saved every one of the richest four hundred taxpayers an average of $46 million per year. Without those tax breaks to the richest four hundred Americans, the U.S. Treasury would have $18 billion more per year.[36] This amount, $18 billion, would pay for more than two years of the federal WIC program that provides healthy food and health care to about nine million poor mothers and their children. Or we could use it to give full Pell Grants ($5,550 each) to over three million more students from lower-income families so they could go to college.

One of the major reasons for the dramatic drop in taxes paid by the richest Americans is that they derive a large portion of their income from capital gains and dividends—both now taxed at only 15%. The richest 1% receives two-thirds of all their income from capital gains and dividends.[37] The top statutory tax rate on capital gains (growth in the value of property,

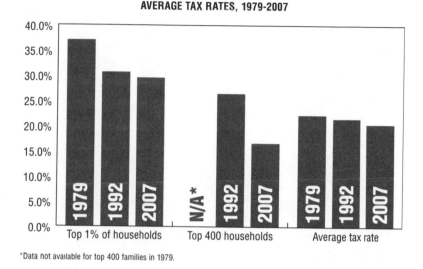

AVERAGE TAX RATES, 1979-2007

*Data not available for top 400 families in 1979.

Figure 2.7. Source: Congressional Budget Office and Internal Revenue Service. www.epi.org/
publication/taxes_on_the_wealthy_have_gone_down_dramatically.

stocks, etc.) has dropped from 39.9% in 1976 to 28% under
President Reagan to 15% under President Bush.[38]

As a result of the tax cuts under President George W. Bush,
the poorest fifth saw their after-tax income increase by $800
per person, but the top fifth enjoyed $8,400 more. And each
filer among the richest 1% benefited by $88,800![39] As figure 2.8
shows, 65% of all the benefits of President Bush's tax cuts went
to the richest 20%. Just the very rich—the top 1%—received
38% of all President Bush's tax cuts. Each of these top 1% had
an annual income of over $600,000 ($620,442 to be exact). Are
they the people that needed more than one-third of all President Bush's tax cuts?

Less progressivity. As a Congressional Research Service report
noted, "Research has shown that the regular income tax has
become less progressive since 1960."[40] A tax is considered "pro-

WHO RECEIVED THE BUSH TAX CUTS

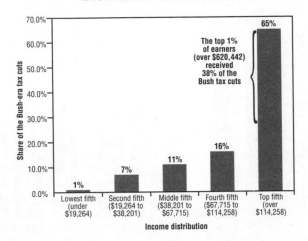

Figure 2.8. Source: Urban-Brookings Tax Policy Center distributional analysis of the 2001-08 tax changes in 2010, measured relative to Clinton-era rates. Income percentile cutoffs are in 2008 dollars. www.epi.org/publication/the_bush_tax_cuts_disproportionately_benefitted_the_wealthy.

gressive" when higher-income folk pay a higher percent in taxes. When the top marginal income tax rate dropped from 91% to 35%, the income tax obviously became less progressive.

Other factors make total federal taxes even less progressive than the income tax. Payroll taxes (for social security and Medicare) raise almost as much money ($864.8 billion in 2010) as federal income taxes ($898.5 billion). But the rich pay the same rate as the poor on the payroll tax (15.3% split between employer and employee until it was temporarily reduced as an economic stimulus). In spite of the fact that the poor pay the same rate as the rich in the payroll tax, we have increased the payroll tax from 6% in the early 1960s to 15.3%. That means that lower-income people today pay a much higher percent of their income on the payroll tax than they did in earlier years. Furthermore, the rich pay much less in relation to their total income. That is partly true because only the first $106,800 of income is subject to the payroll tax and partly because income from investments (e.g., interest, dividends, capital gains)— which make up a much higher percentage of the income of higher-income households—is not subject to the payroll tax at all! So the very wealthy pay a vastly smaller percent of their total income for the payroll tax than do the rest of us. A reduction in the estate tax and dramatic cuts in taxes on capital gains and dividend income also have made total federal taxes far less progressive.

As table 2.2 shows, the richest 20% pay 63.4% of all taxes, but they also make 59% of all the income! This figure also refutes the frequent claim that "the poor don't pay any taxes." It is true that substantial numbers of poorer Americans pay no federal *income* taxes because their total income is so low. But every American who works pays the federal payroll tax. The poor also pay state and local taxes, which are not progressive in the way the federal income tax is. So the poorest fifth pays 16.2% of its total income (the average income per person in 2010 was $12,500) in taxes. The richest 1% pay almost twice as large a percent (30%) of their income in taxes, but they can easily afford it since on average they have an annual income of $1,254,000!

Perhaps Warren E. Buffett is right. Buffett is one of the richest people in the world. But on August 14, 2011, he created a huge stir with a statement in a *New York Times* Op-Ed called "Stop Coddling the Super-Rich." He insisted that mega-rich people like himself should pay more taxes. If we simply returned the average tax rate on the top 1% of taxpayers to its 1996 level (29%) that would raise $100 billion a year. That would be $1 trillion that could go toward reducing the federal deficit in the next decade.[41]

INCOMES AND FEDERAL, STATE AND LOCAL TAXES IN 2010

	Shares of			Taxes as a % of Income		
	Average cash income	Total income	Total taxes	Federal taxes	State & local taxes	Total taxes
Lowest 20%	$ 12,500	3.5%	2.0%	3.9%	12.3%	**16.2%**
Second 20%	25,300	7.1%	5.2%	9.1%	11.6%	**20.7%**
Middle 20%	40,700	11.6%	10.3%	13.9%	11.2%	**25.1%**
Fourth 20%	66,300	19.0%	19.0%	17.3%	11.1%	**28.5%**
Next 10%	100,000	14.3%	15.1%	19.0%	11.0%	**30.0%**
Next 5%	140,000	10.2%	11.2%	20.5%	10.6%	**31.1%**
Next 4%	241,000	14.2%	15.6%	21.4%	9.9%	**31.3%**
Top 1%	1,254,000	20.3%	21.5%	22.1%	7.9%	**30.0%**
ALL	68,200	100.0%	100.0%	18.1%	10.3%	**28.4%**
Addendum: Bottom 99%	$ 56,200	79.8%	78.4%	16.9%	10.9%	**27.9%**

Table 2.2. Source: Institute on Taxation and Economic Policy Tax Model, April 2011. www.ctj.org/pdf/taxday2011.pdf.

TWO CONTRASTING ERAS

There are striking differences between about 1947 and the mid-1970s on the one hand and 1980 to 2010 on the other. In both periods the American economy grew significantly, although it was somewhat more rapid in the earlier era. In the first period, however, the growing wealth benefited all levels of society while in the second it mostly went to the richest 20%. In the first period the top income-tax bracket was high; in the second dramatically lower. In the first period, government made large new investments in education, infrastructure and new social safety nets to protect poorer Americans. In the second period some of those investments weakened. In the first, unions were strong; in the second, much weaker.

It is striking to compare figure 2.9 with figure 2.3. From 1947 to 1979 the income of the bottom four quintiles (i.e., the lower 80%) increased by a higher percent than the top 20%. And the poorest 20% benefited the most! Their income increased 116% while the richest 5% enjoyed a smaller (86%) increase.

The picture is stunningly different for 1979 to 2009. Figure 2.3 (p. 27) shows that in the later period the bottom 20% actually lost ground. The three middle fifths made modest gains, but the top 20% (especially the top 5%) gained by far the most. To a large degree, economic growth for the middle class largely stalled while most of the increased wealth went to the very rich.

The changing share of total pre-tax income enjoyed by the top 1% illustrates this development. Just before the Great Depression, the top 1% (see fig. 2.10) received 23.9% of all

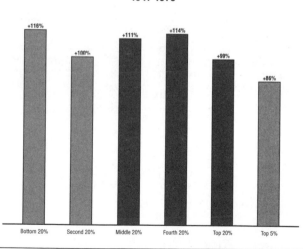

CHANGE IN REAL FAMILY INCOME BY QUINTILE AND TOP 5%, 1947-1979

Figure 2.9. Source: Analysis of U.S. Census Bureau data in Economic Policy Institute, The State of Working America 1994-95 (M. E. Sharpe: 1994), p. 37. http://inequality.org/income-inequality.

income. But in the 1947-1979 period it was much lower at
about 10%, with a low of 8.9% in 1976.[42] Then in the second
period (1979-2009) the richest 1% again took a vastly greater
share of total income—with a peak of 23.5% in 2007 just as
the Great Recession hit.

From about 1945 to 1975, the pay for top executives increased
at less than 1% per year. But from 1980 to 2003, it escalated
about 8 times as fast (6.8% per year).[43]

TOP 1% SHARE OF TOTAL PRE-TAX INCOME, 1913-2008

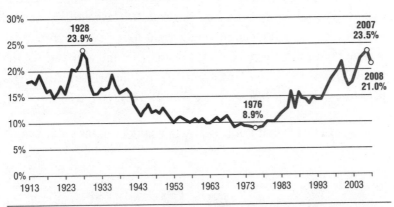

Figure 2.10. Source: Thomas Piketty and Emmanuel Saez, "Income Inequality in the United States,
1913-1998," *Quarterly Journal of Economics* 118(1), 2003. Updated to 2008 at http://emlab.berkeley.
edu/users/saez/. Chuck Marr, "Yes, There's Real Money at the Top," *Off the Charts*, CBPP, August 18,
2011.

Also striking is the fact that the top marginal tax rates were
vastly higher in the first period (70%-90%) than in the second
(35%-39%). Growth in GDP on the other hand was higher on
average per year in the earlier period (about 3.7%) than in the
second (3%).[44]

In the earlier period government invested substantially in education (the GI bill enabled millions of returning World War II
veterans to go to college; government-funded state universities

had low tuition rates); infrastructure (Republican president Eisenhower launched the massive interstate highway system), and health care for elderly and poorer Americans (Medicare and Medicaid). Government mandated a substantial minimum wage (it was $8.68 in 2010 dollars in 1968), helped create the legal and other conditions for labor unions to grow, provided good unemployment insurance, and required employers to pay time-and-a-half for work beyond forty hours a week.[45]

In the second period many of these government programs to support poorer Americans continued. But government decisions helped weaken labor unions, the minimum wage did not keep pace with inflation (in 2010, it was worth only 89% of what it was worth in 1979) and the cost of tuition at state universities increased substantially. As middle-class wages stalled, people borrowed heavily to maintain their spending, which eventually helped produce the Great Recession of 2007.

COMPARING TWO PERIODS

	About 1950-1980	About 1980-2010
Growth in GDP	Faster—annual average of 3.7%	Slower—annual average of 3%
Top tax bracket	High—70%-90%	Much lower—35%-39%
Who benefited?	Poorest 20% received highest percentage income gain (116%) while top 5% gained the least (86%)	Richest 20% gained the most (49% gain in income) while the poorest 20% *lost* 7.4%
Pay for top executives	Slow—less than 1% growth per year	Fast—6.8% growth per year

Table 2.3.

A recent study by the International Monetary Fund (IMF) analyzed the causes of the Great Depression, beginning in 1929, and the Great Recession, starting in 2007. In both cases there was a sharp climb in income inequality and in the level of household debt just before the economic crisis hit. The IMF study argues that the huge growth of inequality in income and wealth was a major cause of both economic disasters.[46] Or, to put it positively, there is a strong positive correlation between greater income equality and better economic growth. In fact, a separate IMF study comparing international economic growth rates found that when inequality decreases by 10%, the length of the period of economic growth increases by 50%.[47]

Not all scholars will agree with the analyses of the IMF study or with my (all too brief) summary of factors that contributed to the differences between the two periods. Nor do I suggest that there were not other important factors that contributed to growing inequality—especially the competition of workers in other countries as economic globalization rapidly increased and technological advances that eliminated many low-skilled but well-paying jobs.[48] What is indisputable is that everyone shared fairly equally in the economic growth of the first period. But in the second, most of the gains went to a small, increasingly rich minority.[49]

The basic facts are clear. Poverty is increasing in America. The richest Americans have vastly increased their share of total income. Our taxes are low—by comparison both with other nations and with other periods of American history. And today's gross inequality is not inevitable, as the comparison with the very different situation in the thirty years before about 1980 clearly shows.

By themselves, however, these central economic facts do not tell us what to do. We also need important moral principles.

3

THE BIG QUESTIONS
IN THE DEBATE

At the very center of today's huge public debate about how to solve our debt crisis lies a cluster of basic questions. Who are persons? Am I responsible for my neighbor? Should we have a special concern for the poor? What is justice? How much inequality is acceptable or desirable? Finally, what is the role of government in overcoming poverty?

Americans—including American evangelicals—offer fundamentally different answers to these foundational questions. I do not pretend that there is any simple biblical answer to all these questions or any easy proof texts that will quickly settle all disagreements. But evangelicals do believe that we should search the Scriptures to develop a biblically grounded framework to approach life today. Therefore I will try to see what biblical principles can guide us in answering these key questions.

WHO ARE PERSONS?

Are you and I primarily isolated individuals? Are we essentially identical peas in some large communal pod? Or are we persons made both for personal freedom and communal interdependence?

The first two answers—radical individualism and communal collectivism—have many adherents. But they are both dangerously wrong.

Radical individualism teaches that persons are fundamentally isolated individuals who can and should make their own personal self-fulfillment their highest value. No American has promoted this view more clearly than the atheist novelist Ayn Rand, whose novel *Atlas Shrugged* has sold over seven million copies in the United States alone. Rand believes that every person is an isolated individual whose value and happiness depend solely on their own individual choices and actions, not on their participation in some larger community. "I don't believe that society has any responsibility to anyone," Rand said.[1] Therefore the highest priority for politics is promoting the total freedom of individuals. Government dare not impose hardly any restrictions on individual choice.

Communal collectivism, the opposite extreme, almost totally subordinates individuals to the larger community. The individual has worth only as a member of the larger whole and must submit all personal interests to it.

There are both ancient and modern versions of communal collectivism: Ancient tribal societies and modern Marxist and fascist totalitarian societies. Both insisted that it is the large collective, not individual persons, that has significance. Political decisions therefore ignore personal freedom and responsibility and subordinate persons to the larger collective, which makes all the important decisions. Any one-sided emphasis on the role of government moves in the direction of this mistake.

Both these positions are fundamentally unbiblical.

Biblical faith combines an amazing personalism with clear communalism. Persons are both free, responsible individuals and also mutually interdependent beings who can only reach the Creator's design for them in vibrant wholesome community.

Nothing affirms the dignity and value of each person as clearly as biblical revelation. Every individual person is created in the image of God (Genesis 1:26-27). Every person is responsible for his or her own choices (Jeremiah 31:29-30; Ezekiel 18:1-4). Jesus insisted that every person must be ready to forsake family ties if necessary to follow him (Matthew 10:34-39). Every single person is summoned to respond to God's offer of salvation and invited to live forever with the living God. A good society, therefore, respects the freedom of individuals. No communal entity dare seek to unconditionally control individual persons.

But the Bible also affirms our communal nature. Adam was restless until he became "one flesh" with Eve. God commanded children to honor parents (Exodus 20:12). When God gave instructions to the people of Israel on how to live well together, he commanded economic sharing: leave part of the harvest for the poor (Deuteronomy 24:19-22); forgive debts every seven years (Deuteronomy 15:1-11); share the tithe with the poor (Deuteronomy 14:28-29; 26:12). When the kingdom of God became powerfully visible in the early church, the first Christians shared economically in such sweeping ways that "there were no needy persons among them" (Acts 4:34). When one suffered, they all suffered (1 Corinthians 12:26).

The deepest foundation of the fact that we are made for community is that we are created in the very image of the trinitarian God—a loving community of three equal but distinct persons who together are one God. The communal aspect of who we are as persons is so important that we simply cannot experience the wholeness that the Creator desires for us as isolated individuals. Living in wholesome community is absolutely essential.

Biblically shaped political engagement will avoid both extremes. It will reject radical individualism and sweeping collectivism. It will embrace a political philosophy that emphasizes freedom for individuals and insists that they take responsibility for their own lives. But it will also demand political decisions that ask individuals to subordinate personal self-interest to the common good.

Closely related to this question, *Who are persons?* is a second hotly debated question: *Am I responsible for my neighbor?*

AM I RESPONSIBLE FOR MY NEIGHBOR?

Ayn Rand and her followers reject the idea that we should sacrifice ourselves for the sake of neighbor. Onkar Ghate, senior fellow at the Ayn Rand Institute in Irvine, California, declares frankly that her philosophy "upholds egoism and individualism," and says each person should pursue "the values that achieve your own individual self-interest and happiness."[2] Self-sacrifice is a vice.[3] Not surprisingly, Ghate candidly admits that "Rand's moral teachings are fundamentally different from Jesus' teachings."

> Ayn Rand and her followers reject the idea that we should sacrifice ourselves for the sake of neighbor.

That is the attitude toward love for neighbor in Rand's highly popular *Atlas Shrugged*. Rand has greatly influenced many important contemporary politicians. Republican congressman Paul Ryan (Chairman of the House Budget Committee) says Ayn Rand is "the reason I got involved in public service." He insists that his staffers read *Atlas Shrugged*.[4] Alan Greenspan, former head of the Federal Reserve Bank, was for a time a member of her inner circle and remained deeply influenced by her ideas. Rand is also widely influential among Tea Party activists.

The opposite extreme toward the neighbor reflects a collectivist mentality. Neighbor love requires that everyone has equal amounts of society's goods. The community is responsible for all neighbors in a way that largely or totally eliminates individual responsibility. Very few people today embrace this extreme position, but substantial tendencies in this direction exist.

Jesus' teaching on love for neighbor is powerful. The second great commandment is "Love your neighbor as yourself" (Luke 10:27). When the rich young ruler asked "Who is my neighbor?" Jesus told the story of the good Samaritan (Luke 10:29-37). The primary point of Jesus' story is that the basic problem is not theoretically figuring out who the neighbor is but actually loving the neighbor. But by making the hated Samaritan the hero who loves even Jews (who despised Samaritans), Jesus is pointedly saying that neighbor love must extend beyond one's own religious and ethnic community. In fact Jesus insists that love for neighbor must even include one's enemies (Matthew 5:43-48). The neighbor to be loved includes the stranger, the imprisoned and the hungry (Matthew 25:31-46). In fact anyone in need is our neighbor. We cannot follow Jesus' teaching without self-sacrifice.

That does not mean that Jesus' teaching on love for neighbor demands total disregard for oneself. In fact Jesus says we should love our neighbor *as ourself.* That means there is a proper regard for oneself.

We cannot follow Jesus' teaching without self-sacrifice.

Genuine love for neighbor also requires that we do what is in the best interest of the neighbor, not what the neighbor asks. When neighbors request what would actually harm them, genuine love for neighbor compels us to refuse their request. That even includes some requests for money—whether that request comes to us personally or through a political process that would provide economic handouts that would undermine personal responsibility and actually harm poor people.

More often, however, the selfishness of well-to-do people discourages them from sacrificially sharing with poor neighbors—whether through personal charity or effective government programs that truly empower poor people. All through the Bible there are literally hundreds of verses that talk about how God's people should imitate God's special concern for the poor (see the next section, "Should We Have Special Concern for the Poor?"). Central to that teaching is the command to share economic resources with needy neighbors.

There is one other aspect of biblical teaching on love for neighbor that is crucial. We do not have identical responsibility for every neighbor in the world. It is probably helpful to think of a set of concentric circles. At the center is family, then the local church, then the global body of Christ, then one's city, then everyone in one's nation and finally everyone in the world. There is no explicit biblical text that says this, but it is a proper implication from what the Bible does say.

At the cross, Jesus asked his disciple John to care for his mother after his death (John 19:25-27). Jesus did not feel obligated to ask John to care for all mothers losing their sons. In his instruction to the church to care for the Christian widows, the apostle Paul says that the first responsibility lies with the widow's family, not the church (1 Timothy 5:3-16). "Anyone who does not provide for their relatives, and especially for their own household, has denied the faith" (v. 8). In a similar way Leviticus 25 says that if a poor person loses his ancestral land, then the "nearest relative" has the first responsibility to help that person recover the land (Leviticus 25:25). And Paul urges Christians to "do good to all people, especially to those who belong to the family of believers" (Galatians 6:10). Proper love for neighbor starts with the family, then the church and finally embraces "all people."

Figure 3.1. The different levels of Christian responsibility

For the Christian, the neighbor we must love—responsibly and self-sacrificially—includes everyone in the world.

SHOULD WE HAVE SPECIAL CONCERN FOR THE POOR?

Ayn Rand represents one extreme response to the question, *Should we have special concern for the poor?* As Michael Gerson, President Bush's speech writer, says of her: "Selfishness is a virtue. Altruism is a crime against human excellence."[5]

Without explicitly embracing Rand's philosophy, many people, including many evangelicals, practice what Rand preaches. They do not share significantly with poor neighbors. And they defend their practice with the argument that they have earned what they have and poor folk should do the same. Helping the poor will only reward irresponsibility and create dependency.

Others seem to think that caring for the poor is the primary Christian virtue. Some liberation theologians have suggested that the only way we know God is through seeking justice for the poor. Jose Miranda, for example, says that God is "knowable *exclusively* in the cry of the poor."[6] For some, working to overcome poverty must be the most important Christian concern. For these folk, concern for sexual integrity, marriage, family, abortion and euthanasia are unimportant.

We should ask the question, *What does the Bible say God cares about?* The answer is quite clear: God cares about the sanctity of human life *and* the poor, the family *and* peacemaking, sexual integrity *and* care for creation. Concern for the poor, however, is one of the most frequently stated biblical demands.

There are literally hundreds and hundreds of biblical verses that emphasize the fact that God and God's faithful people have a special concern for the poor. God acts in history to lift up the poor and cast down those who neglect or oppress them. God identifies with the poor. In fact, those who neglect the poor risk eternal separation from God.[7]

Mary's Magnificat summarizes God's action in history toward the poor: "He has filled the hungry with good things, but has sent the rich away empty" (Luke 1:53). Not only do many texts describe the way God acts in history to lift up the poor, the Bible also teaches pointedly that God actually works in history to pull down those who get rich by oppression or are rich and do not share (e.g., Jeremiah 5:26-29).[8]

Amazingly, the Bible declares that God so identifies with the poor that when we care for the poor and needy, we truly minister to God himself. Proverbs 19:17 declares: "Whoever are kind to the poor lends to the LORD." And Jesus teaches that when we feed the hungry, we actually care for Christ our Lord (Matthew 25:40, 45).

On the other hand, religious people who neglect God's summons to care for the poor are not the people of God at all. God rejects their worship (Isaiah 58:3-7; Amos 5:21-24). Those who do not feed the hungry and clothe the naked go to hell (Matthew 25:44-46). Jeremiah declares that we simply do not know God properly if we do not care for the poor. Speaking of King Josiah, God says:

> God cares about the sanctity of human life *and* the poor, the family *and* peacemaking, sexual integrity *and* care for creation. Concern for the poor, however, is one of the most frequently stated biblical demands.

> He defended the cause of the poor and needy,
>   and so all went well.
> Is that not what it means to know me?
>   declares the LORD. (Jeremiah 22:16)

This text does *not* say that caring for the poor is the *only* way we know God. But it does say that we simply do not know God properly unless, among other things, we actively seek justice for the poor.

Do these hundreds of biblical verses mean God is biased toward the poor? No. The Bible explicitly forbids bias toward the rich or the poor (Leviticus 19:15; Deuteronomy 10:17).

But does God's lack of bias mean that God is neutral in historical situations of injustice? Again, no. Precisely because God cares equally for both oppressor and oppressed, God sides with the oppressed to end the oppression so that oppressed and oppressor may become whole. The analogy of good firefighters helps us understand how God is not biased but sides with the poor. Good firefighters do not spend equal time at every house in the city. They focus on burning houses. But their focus on burning houses does not mean they care more about some people than others.

In a similar way, good parents who love all their children equally do not spend equal time helping the child easily making A's and the one struggling to avoid an F with their homework. They spend more time with the needier child, precisely to be "impartial" and love each child equally.

From one end of the Bible to the other, we hear a powerful summons to have a special concern for poor and needy persons.

God is not biased. But you and I, and almost all comfortable people, are. We care a lot more about ourselves than the poor. But our real bias makes God's lack of bias (God cares equally about everyone) look like a bias.

Precisely because he is not biased, God actively sides with the poor and demands that his faithful people do the same. The biblical God measures societies by what they do to the people at the bottom.

From one end of the Bible to the other, we hear a powerful summons to have a special concern for poor and needy persons.

That is not an option for Christians; it is a crucial criterion of faithfulness. Unless we share God's special concern for the poor, we blatantly disobey the God we worship.

But simply having a concern (even an intense, abiding concern) for the poor is not enough. We also need to know how properly and effectively to empower poor people. Without that, our vigorous efforts may be ineffective or even destructive. To avoid that, we need an answer to the question: What is justice?

WHAT IS JUSTICE?

Some people argue that justice exists if the procedures are fair. No matter what the outcome, no matter how unevenly the goods of society are distributed, justice exists as long as the procedures (e.g., unbiased courts) are fair. According to political philosopher Robert Nozick, justice is whatever emerges from a just situation by just steps. Some evangelicals agree.[9] Evangelical author Cal Beisner, for example, says,

> Such things as minimum wage laws, legally mandated racial quotas in employment, legal restrictions on import and export, laws requiring "equal pay for equal work," and all other regulations of economic activity other than those necessary to prohibit, prevent and punish fraud, theft and violence are therefore unjust.[10]

On the other extreme are Marxists, who argue that justice demands equal outcomes. This means that everyone must have equal amounts of the goods of society: equal income, equal wealth and equal benefits. Marxists even argue that political freedom is irrelevant as long as economic injustice continues. Justice means the equal distribution of society's goods.

There is no biblical treatise with a systematic discussion of the nature of justice. But many different parts of the Bible provide *clues* that help us develop *a biblically informed understanding of justice.*

Three key elements emerge. First, justice is not only procedural but also distributive—it includes outcomes as well as procedures. Second, justice does not require equal outcomes (of income, wealth, etc.), but it does demand that all have access to society's productive resources so that if they act responsibly, they can earn their own way and be dignified members of society. Third, in the case of those unable to earn their own way (children, the elderly, the disabled), justice demands that society provide them with a generous sufficiency.

1. The biblical understanding of justice clearly includes both procedural and distributive aspects. That the procedures must be fair is clear in the several texts that demand unbiased courts (Exodus 23:2-8; Leviticus 19:15; Deuteronomy 1:17; 10:17-19). That distributive justice (i.e., fair outcomes) is also a central part of justice is evident not just from the hundreds of texts about God's concern for the poor (noted in the previous section), but also in the meaning of the key Hebrew words for justice (*mishpat* and *tsedaqah*).

Time and again the prophets use *mishpat* and *tsedaqah* to refer to fair economic outcomes. Immediately after denouncing Israel and Judah for the absence of justice, the prophet Isaiah condemns the way rich and powerful landowners have acquired all the land by pushing out small farmers (Isaiah 5:7-9). It is important to note that even though in this text the prophet does not say the powerful acted illegally, he nevertheless denounces the unfair outcome. In another text Isaiah denounces the powerful who used "unjust laws" to "deprive the poor of their rights" (Isaiah 10:2). The prophet even declares that God will send Israel and Judah into captivity for their economic injustice.

But the prophets also promised that some time in the

future, the Messiah would come to set things right. In that day, they predicted, the Messiah would restore *mishpat* and *tsedaqah*. And that means that everyone will again enjoy their own ancestral land that the powerful had unjustly seized (Isaiah 11:4; Ezekiel 45:8-9; Micah 4:4). The prophets clearly teach that justice includes fair economic outcomes, not just fair procedures.[11]

2. What outcome does justice demand? This issue is *crucial.* The Bible clearly does not endorse the Marxist ideal of equal outcomes. Decisions (good and bad) have consequences that produce economic inequality. Children and grandchildren rightly inherit property (Proverbs 13:22). Laziness produces poverty (Proverbs 10:4). Some inequality of outcome is not only permissible but desirable.

When we examine the Old Testament teaching about the land, a very important norm for distributive justice (fair outcomes) emerges. Israel was an agricultural society, so land was the basic capital, the basic means of producing wealth. God ordained that when Israel moved into the Promised Land, each family would receive an ancestral inheritance sufficient to earn a decent living (Joshua 18; Numbers 26). Then to make sure that no family permanently lost their basic capital to earn their own way, God said that at every Jubilee (the fiftieth year), all land must return to the original owners (Leviticus 25). Furthermore, as we saw earlier, the prophets not only denounced the way the rich and powerful seized the land of poor farmers, they also promised that in the messianic time, everyone would again enjoy their own land so they could earn their own way through productive labor.

This teaching on the land points to a key definition of justice. God wants every person and family to have access to productive resources so that if they act responsibly, they can earn their own way and be dignified members of society. Applying this principle today does not mean some legalistic search for who owned the land fifty years ago. Rather it means applying the basic principle. To do that, we must ask what are the major sources of productive capital in our setting. Land is still one kind of capital. But so is ownership of productive businesses. Knowledge (via education) is probably the most important productive capital in an information society.

Biblical justice rejects the Marxist ideal of equal outcomes just as it rejects limiting justice to fair procedures. But it does demand equality of opportunity up to the point where everyone has access to productive capital so that, if they work responsibly, they can enjoy an adequate income and be dignified members of society.

3. Some people of course—the young, old and disabled—are unable to work. For them the Bible clearly demands that society provide a generous sufficiency.[12] That is also a demand of justice.

The discussion then—on the nature of persons, love for neighbor, our concern for the poor and a definition of justice—provides significant biblical principles for us as we engage current political debates. But two other questions are crucial: (1) If economic equality is not the norm, then how much inequality is acceptable, and when does it become unjust? (2) What is the role of government in empowering the poor and promoting justice? Does responsibility to care for and empower the poor rest only with nongovernmental groups

> God wants every person and family to have access to productive resources so that, if they act responsibly, they can earn their own way and be dignified members of society.

(family, church, etc.)? Or does government have some responsibility? Different answers to both these questions are at the heart of current public debate.

HOW MUCH INEQUALITY IS ACCEPTABLE OR DESIRABLE?

Those who limit justice to fair procedures would place few or no limits on economic inequality. As long as people do not break the law, justice prevails regardless of how rich or poor some people become.

Marxists and many democratic socialists, on the other hand oppose all inequality. The ideal is absolute economic equality.

A **biblical perspective** rejects both of these extremes. As we saw earlier, some inequality is not only permissible but desirable. When laziness and other forms of disobedience result in less income, inequality is appropriate. When parents rightly pass on an inheritance to children and grandchildren, some inequality is appropriate. When the economic rewards of work create incentives for creativity and diligence, some inequality is desirable.

At the same time, biblical principles suggest at least two important limits on economic inequality.

The first concern is the biblical principle that every person and family should have access to adequate productive resources. Whenever the extremes of wealth and income make it difficult or prevent some people from having access to adequate productive capital, then that inequality is unjust and must be corrected. The prophets repeatedly denounced the rich and powerful who acquired more and more land in a way that forced many smaller landowners to lose their land and fall into poverty. One crucial measure for evaluating the economic inequality in a society is to determine whether everyone, especially the poorer members of society, have adequate access to productive resources.

Other things being equal, if a growth in economic inequality has the effect of improving the lot of the poor members of society and increasing their access to productive capital, it is just. On the other hand, any increase in economic inequality that harms the poorer members of society and hinders their opportunity to obtain access to adequate productive capital is unjust.

There is a second key consideration about economic inequality. Especially in a market economy like ours, money is power. And as Lord Acton said long ago, power tends to corrupt and absolute power corrupts absolutely.

The biblical teaching on sin helps explain Lord Acton's dictum. In a fallen world, sinful people will almost always use power for their own selfish advantage. They will use it to abuse others and acquire more power even at the expense of the neighbor.

That is why Christian political thinkers insist on limiting power of every kind. Private ownership limits political power.[13] A democratic political process and the separation of judicial, legislative and administrative branches of government also limit power. In a sinful world, no one, absolutely no one, is to be trusted with unlimited power.

This principle applies to economics just as much as politics. That is why economic monopolies are dangerous, and why having just a handful of huge banks or corporations is dangerous. That is why great economic inequalities will almost always guarantee injustice. One of the most basic principles of historic conservative political thought is that we must avoid unchecked, concentrated power if we want justice and freedom. Great economic inequality inevitably produces injustice in a fallen world. Christians therefore must oppose it.

Even very prominent business leaders sometimes understand the danger of great inequality. Mohamed El-Erian is a pillar of the financial world and CEO of Pimco, one of the world's largest money managers. Recently, he said that the United States must embrace an "inclusive capitalism" and curb excessive inequality. Why? "You cannot be a good house in a rapidly deteriorating neighborhood. The credibility and the fair functioning of the neighborhood matter

> Great economic inequality inevitably produces injustice in a fallen world. Christians therefore must oppose it.

a great deal. Without that, the integrity of the capitalist system will weaken further."[14]

But there is a problem. The previous discussion and principles do not provide a clear formula for saying when the level of economic inequality moves from just and desirable to unjust and dangerous. There is no mathematical formula for that. In every society at every time we must use prudential wisdom to evaluate the level of economic inequality and decide whether and how it must be changed. Honest people will disagree. But if we focus clearly on whether the current level of inequality helps or hinders everyone, especially the poor, to acquire adequate capital and also remember that extremes of power are dangerous, we will be helped to move toward greater justice.

But that still leaves perhaps the most disputed question today: What role should government play in caring for the poor and seeking justice for the needy?

WHAT IS THE ROLE OF GOVERNMENT IN OVERCOMING POVERTY?

Libertarians argue for an extremely limited role for government: primarily just providing a legal framework and organizing the police and national defense. Almost everything else should be left to individuals and private organizations. Government has no responsibility to care for poor people. That is a task for individuals, religious groups and other private charities.

In the summer of 2011 the political action committee of the Family Research Council (a large evangelical public policy organization) ran ads in Kentucky and Ohio opposing government assistance for the poor: "Jesus didn't instruct the government of his day to take the rich young ruler's property and redistribute it to the poor. He asked the ruler to sell his possessions and help the poor. Charity is an individual choice, not a government mandate."[15]

Many evangelicals embrace a libertarian view with regard to helping the poor. (Interestingly, however, evangelicals vigorously—and inconsistently!—reject a libertarian attitude on abortion and marriage, promoting strong governmental action against abortion on demand and supporting heterosexual marriage.)

Many libertarians cite the influence of Ayn Rand, who declared that government has no right "to seize the property of some men for the unearned benefit of others," and that "supporters of the welfare state are morally guilty of robbing their opponents."[16] It is ironic, therefore, that Rand collected government benefits toward the end of her life. After she contracted lung cancer, she applied for Medicare and social security, which she used for the last eight years of her life.[17]

Marxists, on the other hand, want massive government action to guarantee economic equality and thereby (allegedly) end poverty. Government ownership of the means of production, they believe, is the way to do that. While rejecting Marxism, some political liberals seem to think that the first place to look for a solution to any societal problem is government, especially the federal government.

A biblically grounded approach is far more nuanced and

balanced. Good government must be limited government. It dare not undermine crucial nongovernmental institutions such as family, church, business and voluntary organizations. But government also has a significant, although certainly not all-encompassing, responsibility to care for and empower the poor.

Limited government is essential not only because highly concentrated power is dangerous in a sinful world but also because a good, free society consists of many intermediate institutions between individuals and the state. Family, church, other voluntary organizations, business organizations and the like all exist substantially independent of the government and therefore serve to limit the power of government.

All these nongovernmental institutions have central parts to play in preventing poverty and caring for the needy. Strong families play a huge role both in avoiding poverty and in helping poor family members. Private businesses create the vast majority of jobs that enable people to earn a good living. Churches and other voluntary organizations often do a more effective job of assisting poor persons than do government agencies. It would be entirely wrong-headed to look first to government to solve every social problem, including poverty.

But this is not to suggest that government has no significant role to play in combating poverty. The libertarian view that government has no responsibility to care for and empower the poor flies in the face of clear biblical teaching.

First Kings 10:9 says of King Solomon: The Lord "has made you king to maintain justice and righteousness." Psalm 72:1 is a prayer for the leader of the government: "Endow the king with your justice, O God, the royal son with your righteousness." And Jeremiah declares that good king Josiah knew God because he "did what was right and just. . . . He defended the cause of the poor and needy" (Jeremiah 22:15-16).

Central to biblical teaching about the king is the responsibility to do "righteousness and justice." Each of the three passages just cited use the key Hebrew words (or their derivatives):
mishpat and *tsedaqah*. As we saw earlier, these words refer to
both fair judicial procedures (procedural justice) and just economic outcomes (distributive justice). These two tasks of procedural and distributive justice correspond to a substantial
degree to the explicit New Testament teaching that government
has the double task of restraining evil and promoting the good
(Romans 13:4; 1 Peter 2:13-14). Government cares for the poor
both by restraining powerful evil people and by assisting and
empowering the poor.

After praying that God will give the king God's justice, the
psalmist goes on to say:

He will defend the afflicted among the people
    and save the children of the needy;
    he will crush the oppressor.
        (Psalm 72:2-4; cf. Ecclesiastes 4:1)

In a similar way, Jeremiah says that king Josiah "defended
the cause of the poor and needy and so all went well" (Jeremiah
22:16). There are wicked, powerful people in society who oppress the poor. One role of government is to protect the poor
from these powerful (nongovernmental!) oppressors.

But the biblical material in no way restricts the role of government to operating fair courts that defend the poor. Many
texts talk about the way the rulers assist the poor and promote
economic justice.

Central to economic justice and the avoidance of poverty in
the Old Testament vision is the understanding that the land
(the basic capital in an agricultural society) was divided up so
that every family had their own land. And the leader Joshua

led the people in this decentralized division of the land (Joshua 18:1-10). Furthermore, in order to help avoid the emergence of persistent poverty among the people of Israel, God commanded that debts should be forgiven every seven years (Deuteronomy 15:1-11) and that every family should return to their ancestral land every fifty years, regardless of why they lost their land (Leviticus 25). In neither case is there any suggestion that forgiveness of debts or the Jubilee was a voluntary act that individuals were free to practice or ignore. It was God's law—and presumably the rulers were supposed to lead in the implementation.

As we saw earlier, the prophets also predicted a messianic time when justice would prevail and everyone would again enjoy their own land (Micah 4:4; Zechariah 3:10). In his vivid depiction of this messianic restoration of ancestral land, Ezekiel denounces the rulers for wrongly seizing people's land and predicts that the rulers will finally play their proper role in helping everyone enjoy their productive capital (Ezekiel 45:1-10, esp. vv. 8-9).

Nehemiah 5 contains a striking account of the governor (the top government official in Judah) denouncing powerful Jews who were oppressing their own people. Nehemiah demanded that they promptly return the land of the poor. Judah was a province of Persia, but the Persian ruler had appointed Nehemiah as governor of Judah and allowed him to rebuild Jerusalem. After some time, however, Nehemiah discovered that powerful Jews were oppressing their fellow Jews. Because of famine, poor Jews had mortgaged and then lost their fields in order to buy food. Others had sold their children into slavery. Rich, powerful Jews were profiting from the desperate situation of the poor.

Furious, Nehemiah called a public assembly and denounced

the powerful Jewish oppressors. "Give back to them immediately their fields, vineyards, olive groves and houses, and also the interest you are charging them," Nehemiah demanded (Nehemiah 5:11). The rich oppressors agreed and Nehemiah made them take an oath to keep their promise. Nehemiah did not wait for the next Jubilee to demand that the rich return the land of the poor so that they could again earn their own way. As the ruler, he insisted that the poor immediately recover their productive capital.

In a careful article on the various Old Testament provisions to care for the very poor (e.g., no interest loans, the third-year tithe for the poor), Christian economist John Mason asked whether these provisions were only suggestions for voluntary charity or laws to be enforced by the leadership of the community:[18]

> The third-year tithe was gathered in a central location (Deuteronomy 14:28) and then shared with the needy. Community leaders would have had to act together to carry out such a centralized operation. In the Talmud, there is evidence that the proper community leaders had the right to demand contributions. Nehemiah 5 deals explicitly with the violations of these provisions on loans to the poor. The political leader calls an assembly, brings "charges against the nobles," and commands that the situation be corrected (Neh. 5:7 NRSV; cf. all of vv. 1-13). Old Testament texts often speak of the "rights" or "cause" of the poor. Since these terms have clear legal significance, they support the view that the provisions we have explored for assisting the poor would have been legally enforceable. "The clear fact is that most provisions for the impoverished were part of the Mosaic legislation, as much as other laws such as those dealing with murder and theft. Since nothing in the text

allows us to consider them as different, they must be presumed to have been legally enforceable."[19]

Some may argue that these Old Testament passages apply only to the ancient people of Israel and therefore are not relevant for today. But that is mistaken. The Old Testament ideal is for the king to be a channel of God's justice (Psalm 72:1), and God's justice extends to the whole earth (Psalm 9:7-9). All legitimate rulers are instituted by God and are to be God's servants for good (Romans 13:1, 4).

Daniel 4:27 demonstrates that the ideal of the king as the protector of the weak has universal application. God demands that the Babylonian monarch no less than the Israelite king "renounce your sins by doing what is right, and your wickedness by being kind to the oppressed" (Daniel 4:27 NRSV). Similarly in Proverbs 31:9, King Lemuel (generally considered to be a northern Arabian monarch) is called to "defend the rights of the poor and needy."

There is at least one other major consideration that supports the claim that government has a significant role in empowering the poor. Poverty results both from wrong personal choices and unfair systems. The prophets denounced unfair legal and economic systems that produce poverty (Isaiah 5:8-9; Amos 2:6-7; 5:10-15). Isaiah 10:1-2 very explicitly says that sometimes rulers make unjust laws to oppress the poor: "Woe to those who make unjust laws . . . to deprive the poor of their rights and withhold justice from the oppressed of my people." Equally bluntly, Psalm 94:20 denounces a throne "that brings on misery by its decrees."

Government legislation sometimes produces or nurtures unjust, oppressive structures that destroy the poor (e.g., legalized slavery). Just as clearly, good governmental legislation (e.g., the abolition of slavery) can encourage more just structures that truly empower the poor and oppressed. The return of ancestral land every fifty years was a structural policy for empowering the poor, not a voluntary act of charity.

"For the Health of the Nation," the unanimously approved official public policy document of the National Association of Evangelicals (which represents 30 million evangelicals in the United States), clearly affirms the importance of wise governmental action to promote structures that empower the needy:

> From the Bible, experience, and social analysis, we learn that social problems arise and can be substantially corrected by both personal decisions and structural changes. On the one hand, personal sinful choices contribute significantly to destructive social problems (Prov. 6:9-11), and personal conversion through faith in Christ can transform broken persons into wholesome, productive citizens. On the other hand, unjust systems also help create social problems (Amos 5:10-15; Isa. 10:1-2) and wise structural change (for example legislation to strengthen marriage or increase economic opportunity for all) can improve society. Thus Christian civic engagement must seek to transform both individuals and institutions. While individuals transformed by the gospel change surrounding society, social institutions also shape individuals. While good laws encourage good behavior, bad laws and systems foster destructive action. Lasting social change requires both personal conversion and institutional renewal and reform.[20]

A couple statistics underline the importance of governmental action to care for the poor. In the United States today tens of millions of poor people need food assistance each month. There are thousands of voluntary organizations lovingly providing important food aid. But of all the food assistance provided each month in the United States, 94% comes from government. A mere 6% comes from private sources.[21]

Today, there are five major federal government antipoverty programs: SNAP (food stamps), TANF (welfare), Earned Income Tax Credit (a tax credit to enhance the income of the working poor), SSI (assistance for the disabled) and Medicaid (healthcare). In 2010 these five programs cost the federal government about $485 billion.[22] If the 325,000 religious congregations in the United States wished to take over these programs, each congregation would need to add about $1.5 million to its annual budget. Any problem for your congregation?

Even as politically conservative a person as theologian Wayne Grudem, he still argues that government should provide a "safety net" "to keep people from going hungry or without clothing or shelter." He also believes that "it is appropriate for government to provide funding so that everyone is able to *gain enough skills and education to earn a living.*"[23]

There is no basis in biblical thought to argue that government should have no role in caring for and empowering poor people. That is not to say that government should automatically be the first place we go to combat poverty. We should always ask if we can achieve better results in reducing poverty by strengthening families, encouraging private charitable organizations and encouraging businesses to create

> Of all the food assistance provided each month in the United States, 94% comes from government.

more jobs. Sometimes, however, government must step in precisely because other societal institutions fail to do what they should or because they lack the resources or the authority to do what is needed.

And sometimes the government, indeed the federal government, is the most effective place to solve a particular problem. If we leave the issue of employers paying a fair wage solely to individual businesses, then the business that pays lower wages will often enjoy a comparative advantage and drive out of business those firms that seek to pay a living wage. Similarly, if we leave this issue to individual cities or states, then their corporations may leave for other places without a minimum wage law. Some things can only be done effectively at the level of the federal government.

The answers to our six basic questions do not instantly solve today's political debates about how to solve the debt crisis. We also need accurate economic information about many things. But the fundamental, biblically grounded principles outlined in this chapter will provide crucial guidance as we sort through the economic-political options.

4

CURRENT PROPOSALS

Simply Not Good Enough

There is no quick fix to our country's deficit crisis. It cannot be solved in a year or two—or even five. We must begin to make crucial decisions now. But Christian citizens must prepare to struggle with this problem for years.

To do that wisely we need some basic criteria for evaluating the current proposals—and the new ones that will emerge year after year. Both foundational principles and more concrete, prudential norms are necessary.

PRINCIPLES AND NORMS

Seven foundational principles. Key principles emerged in chapter three from our study of relevant biblical/theological truths.

1. In our understanding of persons we must hold together two truths: persons are made both for personal freedom and responsibility, and for communal interdependence. Radical individualism and sweeping collectivism are both fundamental mistakes.

2. We do have responsibility for our neighbors. Jesus com-

mands us to love our neighbor as ourselves. But genuine love for neighbor requires not unending handouts but a tough love that does what is in the genuine long-term interest of the neighbor.

3. God and God's faithful people have a special concern for the poor. Since God measures societies by what they do to the people on the bottom, we must evaluate proposals to end the deficit crisis by what they do to the poorer members of society.

4. Justice does not demand equal income and wealth, but it does require that everyone has access to the productive resources (land, capital, education) so that, when they act responsibly, they will be able to earn an adequate living and be respected members of society. It also requires that those unable to work (children, the disabled, the elderly) enjoy a generously sufficient living.

5. Economic equality is not a biblical norm. But economic inequality that harms the poorer members of society and prevents them from gaining access to productive resources (e.g., quality education) is wrong. Furthermore, economic inequality that places most of the political power in the hands of a few will almost inevitably lead to great injustice.

6. Government is only one of many crucial institutions in society, and its power must be limited. But in biblical teaching, there is a significant, legitimate role for government in caring for the poor and promoting economic opportunity. It is simply unbiblical to claim that caring for the poor is only a responsibility of individuals and private organizations but not the government.

7. Intergenerational justice is important. One generation should not benefit or suffer unfairly at the cost of another. Scripture

clearly teaches that parents should act in ways that help their children to flourish (Deuteronomy 6:7; Psalm 78:4; Joel 1:3). To continually place current expenditures on our children's and grandchildren's credit cards is flatly immoral.

Seven more concrete, prudential norms. As we start with these principles and then carefully study our world (especially its economics and politics), several other prudential norms emerge. I do not claim the same authority for the following *seven* norms as I do for the preceding principles. But I do think these norms are grounded in moral truth and careful societal analysis. And they are helpful as we evaluate proposals to reduce the budget deficit.

1. We must keep and strengthen effective programs that serve and empower poor people. This norm is simply a restatement in a more concrete form of principle three about God's concern for the poor.

In the course of 2011 a wide range of Christian leaders urged the government to observe this norm. The board of directors for the National Association of Evangelicals (which represents the largest group of U.S. evangelicals) passed a resolution called "Lowering the Debt, Raising the Poor." The NAE believes smart, cost-effective programs to help those in poverty should be maintained and strengthened.[1] The Catholic bishops said the same thing in an April 13, 2011, letter to the House of Representatives: "The needs of those who are hungry and homeless, without work or in poverty should come first." In April of 2011 I joined a large number of religious leaders who came together to form a "Circle of Protection" to promote this norm (see chap. 5, p. 138).

It is important to note—as many different people have pointed out—that a whole series of successful deficit reduction packages and automatic budget-cut mechanisms passed by the Congress in the last quarter century have exempted key programs for low-income people. This was true under both Republican (Reagan and the first Bush) and Democratic (Clinton) presidents. In fact, in 1990, under the first President Bush, and in 1993 under President Clinton, the deficit-reduction legislation actually increased the Earned Income Tax Credit, which lifted millions out of poverty.[2] In the 1993 package there were increases in food stamps. And the 1997 legislation created CHIP—a major health program for poor children. Past history proves that it is possible both to shrink the deficit and reduce poverty.

Even the politically conservative Heritage Foundation recognizes that we should protect effective programs that empower poor people. Stuart Butler, director of the Center for Policy Innovation at the Heritage Foundation, says: "Few would support the idea that the poor should endure the same budget axe that everybody else must endure in these difficult times."[3]

2. We should cut ineffective, duplicative and wasteful programs. Not all programs to assist the needy actually work. We also have duplicative programs, in different federal departments. In 2010 the federal government ran more than forty-four different job-training programs, operated by nine different federal agencies. And there were at least twenty programs in twelve different agencies studying invasive species![4] There may be a good reason for keeping some of these different programs, but many of them should be consolidated.

The Government Accountability Office has discovered that the Pentagon spent $295 billion in cost overruns on ninety-five weapons systems.[5]

Republican Senator Tom Coburn issued a "Wastebook" with a list of one hundred ridiculous federal expenditures totaling $11.5 billion. He comments, "well-intentioned people across the political spectrum will argue about the best way to get us back on track. But we can all agree that cutting wasteful and low priority spending from the budget is not only sensible, but essential."[6] People who care about the poor should take the lead in demanding an end to ineffective, duplicative and wasteful programs.

3. Everyone should contribute, but those with the most resources should contribute the most. It is impossible to solve the deficit crisis simply by increasing taxes on the richest. But as megabillionaire Warren Buffett has said, the richest Americans should contribute more. A poll in the spring of 2011 found that almost two-thirds (66%) of all Americans think it is fair for more-wealthy people to pay more taxes than poorer or middle-class folk. Fifty-eight percent of Republicans and even half (49%) of Tea Party people agree.[7] The widely cited report of the bipartisan National Commission on Fiscal Responsibility and Reform (December 2010), chaired by Republican Senator Alan Simpson and Democrat Erskine Bowles insisted that "those of us who are best off will need to contribute the most." And they concluded that we must "maintain or increase progressivity in the tax code."[8]

4. We must include the defense budget as we cut federal expenditure. Currently, the United States spends about as much on military expenditures as all other nations combined.[9] Both of the two major bipartisan reports on deficit reduction insist that cuts in the defense budget are essential.[10]

5. We should continue to invest in education, infrastructure and research. As the bipartisan commission led by Simpson and Bowles insists, we need better-educated Americans, improved infrastructure, such as roads and bridges, and high-value research if our economy is to grow.[11] Thomas Donohue, president and CEO of the U.S. Chamber of Commerce, said in late 2011 that their recent research has shown that poor transportation infrastructure is costing the U.S. economy a great deal. Improving this infrastructure, he said, "could unlock $1 trillion in economic potential, . . . boost productivity and economic growth in the long run and support millions of jobs in the near term."[12]

6. **We should adopt a roughly equal (50-50) mix between increased revenue and cuts in spending.**[13] In fact, the budget deals of President Reagan in 1982 and 1984 increased taxes a lot more than they cut expenditures.[14] Both by American historical standards and international standards, American tax rates are low. Increasing federal taxes by a couple percentage points of GDP will not produce a dangerously powerful federal government.

7. **We should move decisively (but not instantly) to substantially reduce and then largely end budget deficits.** Federal Reserve Board Chairman Bernanke said in July 2011 that the United States should not immediately adopt large deficit reduction measures because the economy is still too fragile.[15] Simpson-Bowles said the same.[16] But we must set a clear target for a reasonable level of federal debt. A study by the Congressional Research Service of many of the major deficit reduction proposals noted that they all agree that by 2020, the publicly held national debt should be no higher than 60% of GDP.[17]

These principles and norms provide criteria for judging the ongoing stream of proposals for deficit reduction. The rest of this chapter uses them to evaluate major proposals advanced in 2011. But they will apply equally to the future debate and ever-new proposals over the next five and more years.

2011 PROPOSALS

A comparison of the budget proposals for fiscal year 2012 (FY2012) made by Democratic President Obama on the one hand and the one passed by the Republican-controlled House of Representatives on the other offer both significant similarities and striking contrasts. Neither measures up to the criteria just outlined.

The fiscal year for the federal government runs from October 1 to September 30. By early February of each year the President must propose a budget for the following year. The House and Senate ought to agree on a series of appropriations bills and send them to the President to sign before the fiscal year begins, but this deadline is regularly missed.

In very early February 2011, President Obama released his budget for FY2012. On April 5, Rep. Paul Ryan, the chair of the House Budget Committee, presented the Republican FY2012 budget (often called the Ryan budget). On April 7 the Republican Study Committee (a caucus of 170 conservative Republicans in the House) offered their own FY2012 budget. On April 15 the Republican-controlled House passed the Ryan budget. On September 8, President Obama presented a stimulus bill and on September 19, he unveiled additional plans to reduce the deficit. Comparing and contrasting these Democratic and Republican proposals will illustrate two different approaches to fixing the budget deficit.

Ryan budget. New York Times columnist David Brooks (one of my favorite columnists) wrote that the Ryan budget was bold and courageous.[18] Ryan deserves credit for daring to tackle the tough problem of escalating federal health care costs in Medicare and Medicaid whether or not we agree with his concrete proposals. But the Ryan budget drastically cut important programs that protect low-income people, failed to cut the defense budget and offered still more tax cuts to the richest Americans.

Over the next ten years the Ryan budget cut $1.6 trillion in nonsecurity discretionary programs.[19] A quarter of this, or $400 billion, is estimated to come from various programs

serving low- and moderate-income families and communities—
for example, cuts in things like low-income housing assistance,
early childhood education, community development, cash assistance and supplemental nutrition programs. It also cuts $127
billion from the federal food stamp program (called SNAP),
which currently provides food aid to more than 44 million
Americans. Another $126 billion in cuts to educational, training
and employment-related services would likely come mainly
from Pell Grants that help children from lower-income families
go to college.[20] The Ryan budget also proposes large cuts in
economic foreign aid.[21]

The Ryan budget also included drastic cuts in health care
programs that help the poor and elderly: Medicaid, Medicare
and CHIP.

Medicaid provides money to the states so they can offer
health care for more than 58 million poor Americans, including
almost 30 million children. It also covers nursing care for poor
elderly folk and health care for those with disabilities. The Ryan
budget cut $771 billion from Medicaid over ten years. According
to the Congressional Budget Office, it would cut federal funding
by 35% in 2022 and by 49% in 2030—at a time when both the
numbers needing this help and the cost of health care are constantly rising.[22] Millions of poor Americans would go without
adequate health care.

The Ryan budget would also radically change Medicare—
health care for seniors. Instead of the current program that
guarantees financial access to good health care for all seniors,
the program would be converted to a voucher program to help
each senior purchase private health insurance. But private
health insurance costs more per person than the current
federal Medicare program. Furthermore, the vouchers would
not rise as fast as projected health care costs. Based on Con-

gressional Budget Office cost estimates, by 2022 the cost that the average elderly person would have to pay from their own pocket would double, increasing from $6,150 to $12,500. And in later years, as the value of the vouchers eroded, it would be even more.[23]

In addition, the Ryan budget would have repealed the 2010 Affordable Care Act—and thus eliminated the expansion of health insurance for the approximately 30 million uninsured Americans that would soon receive coverage under that legislation.

Almost two-thirds of all the cuts in the Ryan budget came from programs that help lower-income people.[24] At the same time, the Ryan budget slightly increased the military budget. And even while dramatically cutting effective programs for poor people it added further tax cuts for the richest Americans!

The Ryan budget would make permanent all the Bush-era tax cuts, even though 65% of all those tax cuts went to the richest 20%, and 38% went just to the top 1% (see fig. 2.10). It would also lower the top income-tax rate from 35% to 25%. Almost all the benefits for this change would go to the richest 5% of taxpayers! Ninety-five percent of all Americans would receive no direct benefits from lowering the top rate. The Ryan budget does plan to close some tax loopholes (although they remain unspecified), but every dollar raised that way goes for tax cuts that almost totally benefit the wealthy. Apparently tax cuts for the rich matter more than reducing the deficit.

Moreover, with all the Ryan budget's tax cuts for the rich (causing an estimated $4.2 trillion loss in revenue),[25] the Congressional Budget Office says that, under it, the debt would actually increase by 8% over the next ten years. Under the Ryan budget the federal budget would go on adding to the debt until sometime in the mid 2030s.[26] That is not good enough.

Even more drastic would be the cuts in programs for poor

Americans if the proposed budget of the Republican Study Committee were adopted. This committee represents a large majority (170) of all Republicans in the House of Representatives. Their proposed budget would add no new federal revenue. But it cut in *half* by 2021 food stamps (SNAP), Medicaid and Supplemental Security Income (SSI). Currently, SSI provides

RYAN'S PROPOSED BUDGET FY2012

Proposed Areas of Change	Proposed Action
Cuts	
• Food stamps (SNAP)	*cut* $127 billion
• Pell Grants	*cut* tens of billions of dollars
• WIC	*cut* $733 million
• Medicaid	*cut* $771 billion (35% by 2022)
• Medicare	*cut* and privatize
• New (2010) Health Insurance for 30 million uninsured	*cut* totally
Increases	
• Defense Budget	increased by $200 billion over ten years
• New Tax cuts for rich	richest 5% get 95% of new tax cuts
• Federal debt	increased by 8% over 10 years.

Table 4.1.

benefits to poor people who are elderly or severely disabled, and it raises their income to about 75% of the poverty level. This budget would cut those benefits in half by 2021. Food stamps (SNAP) would lose $350 billion—50%—over ten years. Medicaid would lose 54% of its funding by 2021.[27] The military budget would increase.[28]

President Obama's proposals. Although President Obama's proposals are fairly similar to those of Congressman Ryan in some areas, they differ fundamentally in many others.[29] Especially important are the areas of Medicare, Medicaid and major programs to help poor people.

In the area of the military budget, Ryan's and Obama's proposals do not differ dramatically, although Obama chose zero growth for five years while Ryan increased the military budget modestly every year from 2010 to 2021.[30] This would mean, according to Reuters (a global news service), that the Ryan budget would add about $200 billion in defense spending over ten years, and Obama's budget would bring a relatively modest cut of $400 billion over the same period.[31] A difference of $600 billion is not insignificant. But Obama's cuts are not enough for a defense budget that is currently as large as all the rest of the world's defense budgets combined.

Both cut agricultural subsidies significantly.[32] And both cut benefits for federal employees, although Ryan made much deeper cuts than did Obama.[33]

On programs for low-income people, Medicare, Medicaid and taxes, on the other hand, the two sets of proposals differed dramatically.

Obama made no cuts to most of the federal programs supporting low-income folk. There were no cuts to food stamps (SNAP), child nutrition programs and Supplemental Security Income (SSI).[34] Nor did he propose cuts in foreign economic aid that helps the poorest around the world.

Whereas the Ryan budget cut Medicaid (the major health care program for poor Americans) by $771 billion over ten years, Obama sought to reduce it by only about $70 billion.[35]

The difference in Medicare is equally stark. Rejecting the Ryan budget's plan to change Medicare to a voucher program, Obama sought to retain the current structure of Medicare, which guarantees financial access to good health care for all seniors. At the same time, Obama would cut $248 billion from the growth of Medicare in the next ten years with several changes. These include requiring drug companies to provide further discounts for prescriptions for poor Americans and increasing the premiums for higher-income Americans.[36]

Whereas the Ryan budget proposed substantial new tax cuts for the richest Americans, President Obama picked up Warren Buffett's call for higher taxes on very rich people. Obama's mix of spending reductions and tax increases are not what I consider wise. The program cuts are much larger than the increases in income. But he does recognize that to solve our deficit crisis, we must have both.

There are also important things to criticize in President Obama's proposals.

Obama's deficit reduction proposals are not good enough. According to the U.S. Office of Management and Budget, under Obama's plans outlined in his FY2012 budget, the national debt would increase by $7.205 trillion in the next ten years![37] President Obama offered additional proposals for deficit reduction on September 19, 2011, and the $2 trillion in savings over ten years would stabilize the debt for one decade. But his proposals do not stabilize the debt after that. "This is just not enough," commented the president of the bipartisan Committee for a Responsible Federal Budget.[38]

One major reason Obama's deficit reduction proposals are inadequate is because he is unwilling to get even close to a 50-50 mix of tax increases and programs cuts. A White House press release on April 13, 2011, said the President sought a "balanced approach" of three dollars in spending cuts for every one dollar in increased tax revenues.[39] One major reason Obama does not adopt a 50-50 mix is that since his run for President he has promised not to raise taxes on anyone except those making more than $250,000 a year. As USA Today pointed out in a recent editorial, that is ridiculous. The 2011 budget deficit is about $1.3 trillion. Even if we doubled the taxes on the richest 1%, that would only close about one quarter ($350 billion) of the deficit gap.[40] The richest Americans should pay significantly more taxes, but many more of us will also need to contribute.

President Obama has failed to embrace a wise reform proposed by Republican leader Paul Ryan. One significant (although not primary) reason medical costs have increased is because lawsuits against doctors for malpractice have dramatically increased medical malpractice insurance. Persons should be able to sue doctors for economic losses that their medical mistakes have caused. But courts have given very high awards for noneconomic and punitive damages. The Ryan budget rightly sought to limit awards for noneconomic and punitive damages.[41] So did the Fiscal Commission President Obama appointed.[42] Unfortunately, Democrats oppose this change in part because so many of the lawyers who bring these lawsuits are Democratic supporters.

Also unwise is President Obama's proposal to substantially reduce the deduction for charitable donations for high-income taxpayers.[43] One good aspect of American society is the way that large charitable donations support a wide range of organi-

PRESIDENT OBAMA'S PROPOSED BUDGET FY2012

Proposed Areas of Change	Proposed Action
Cuts	
• Defense budget	• $400 billion over 10 years
• Medicaid	• Modest cut of about $70 billion over 10 years
• Medicare	• Keep present system with modest cuts
• Tax deduction for charitable donations by rich	($248 billion over 10 years)
	• Reduction in amount of deduction allowed
No Cuts	
• Food stamps (SNAP)	
• Child Nutrition Program	
• SSI for disabled	
• Economic foreign aid	
Increases	
• Taxes on richest	Modest increases
• National debt	Increase by $7.2 trillion in 10 years

Table 4.2.

zations in civil society. The fact that donors receive a tax break for these donations encourages giving. We should not remove that incentive to nurture a vigorous civil society.

Clearly, both the Republican and the Democratic proposals offered in 2011 are inadequate. Equally obvious is the fact that they point to fundamentally different paths. Should we slash programs for poor Americans, increase the military budget and offer more large tax cuts to the richest Americans?

In chapter five I offer what I believe is a better solution.

5

A BETTER WAY

Now comes the hard part. We must move decisively to stop never-ending budget deficits without slashing effective programs that offer life, health and opportunity to poor neighbors.[1] We also must move quickly, but not in ways that cause another recession. We should promptly signal a change in policies while recognizing that many deficit-reduction measures should wait until the economy is stronger to avoid harming the fragile economic recovery.

Accomplishing all this would be difficult in any political context. In the current setting of almost total political gridlock it often feels impossible. But we dare not surrender to despair. If I had no hope, I would not have bothered to write this book! Over my lifetime, I have seen seemingly impossible situations change for the better. The Civil Rights movement's successful struggle against racism, the victory over apartheid in South Africa, the emergence of dozens of new democratic governments in the past few decades and the astonishing events of the Arab Spring in 2011 all inspire hope.

Thank God we still have a free democratic system even though wealthy people have vastly more political influence than ordinary citizens. But if a large number of people organize and demand change, things can improve. I am certain that if just 10% of Americans would commit themselves to an organized, sustained ten-year struggle for economic justice, we could end the deficit crisis, promote intergenerational justice for our grandchildren and strengthen the poorest among us. Biblical Christians, I hope and pray, will lead the way in fixing the moral deficit.

But what should we do? What concrete agenda flows from the principles and norms and factual data we have explored?

Six areas are especially important:

• programs that assist and empower poor people

• farm programs

• the tax code

• social security for seniors

• health care

• national defense

What do we need to do in each of these areas to both end the deficit crisis and promote justice, both for the poor and our grandchildren?

ASSISTING AND EMPOWERING POOR NEIGHBORS

Not all programs designed to help the poor are effective.[2] We need to end programs that do not work. But we also should continue—and even expand—effective programs that prevent hunger, poor health and death, and empower people to acquire the knowledge and resources to be healthy, productive members of society. We will probably also need to create new effective programs to replace discarded programs that sought to solve real problems but proved to be ineffective.

Both morality and economics demand such action. Cutting effective programs that reduce hunger, disease and death denies the most basic truth about persons—the fact that every person is created in the image of God and is of inestimable value to the living God. To be pro-life is to be pro-poor.

It is also economically foolish to slash effective programs that reduce poverty. If a poor, pregnant mother lacks basic nutrition and health care, her child is far more likely to have chronic health problems and require expensive medical care. Disadvantaged children without adequate food and good early childhood education do poorly and then drop out of school, become unemployed or go to jail. If we do not invest in poor children and their families, we are less likely to see them become productive, tax-paying citizens. Advocating short-term savings that produce far more long-term expenses is economically foolish.

So what are the kinds of programs we should maintain and strengthen? I cannot, of course, discuss every effective program. Instead I will describe some of the most significant.

Domestic programs. Food stamps (SNAP). In May of 2011, 45 million Americans received food stamps. (The official name of the program is Supplemental Nutrition Assistance Program, SNAP for short). To receive food stamps, a household's gross income must be below 130% of the poverty level. In 2010 that would have meant an upper limit of $23,800 for a family of three. The actual amount of the assistance varies depending on food prices and the family's income. In 2010 the average was $4.46 per day per person.[3]

Fully half of all Americans will receive help from SNAP before they are twenty years old. Yes, that is not a typo. Fifty percent of Americans will benefit from food stamps sometime before they are twenty. For African Americans the figure is

90%.[4] In 2009, 41% of everyone receiving SNAP benefits lived on income 50% less than the poverty level—that is, $10,220 for the whole year for a family of four! Any volunteers? Anybody who thinks these neighbors should not receive help to buy food?

SNAP is a mandatory program. That means that everyone who meets the criteria is eligible to receive help. That also means that the cost of SNAP varies from year to year depending on the economy. That is why the number of people receiving SNAP benefits jumped enormously during the recent recession. In 2009 the number increased by 25% to more than 33 million people. In 2010 it climbed to 40 million, and in 2011 it rose to over 45 million—one in seven Americans.[5]

The Ryan budget said this program was experiencing "relentless and unsustainable growth" and proposed to cut SNAP expenditures by $127 billion over ten years.[6] In fact, the SNAP program worked exactly as it should during the terrible economic collapse of the Great Recession when millions of additional people became eligible for this essential program. The recession is the major reason SNAP costs grew by 102% between 2007 and 2010.[7] Between 2007 and 2010 an additional 6.3 million Americans fell into poverty. But the Congressional Budget Office predicts that as the economy strengthens and unemployment levels fall, the number of people using SNAP and the costs of the program will drop substantially.[8]

Nor does SNAP create long-term dependency. A study by the U.S. Department of Agriculture found that half of all SNAP participants remained in the program for eight months or less. When their immediate need passed, they left the program.[9]

SNAP is a well-run, effective program. Every dollar spent on SNAP benefits produces an additional $1.74 of economic activity during periods when the economy is weak. The SNAP program has one of the best quality-control systems of all public benefit programs, and in recent years its error rates have dropped to an all-time low. In 2009 the net loss to errors was only 2.7% of total program costs.[10]

Furthermore, SNAP dramatically reduces poverty. It lifts more families with children out of poverty than any other federal program except the Earned Income Tax Credit.[11] The Census Bureau reported that in 2010 SNAP lifted 3.9 million people (including 1.7 million children) out of poverty.[12]

SNAP works effectively. It should be strengthened, not cut.

Women, Infants and Children (WIC). WIC provides healthy food, counseling on good eating habits and access to health care to about 9 million low-income pregnant and postpartum women, infants and children (under age five) who are at risk of poor nutrition.[13] Federal costs in 2010 were $6.7 billion.[14]

Extensive study over the past twenty years has shown that WIC reduces low birth rates and infant mortality. Women who participate in WIC have healthier babies, and their children achieve higher IQ scores.[15] And it is cost effective. One landmark study discovered that for every dollar spent on WIC, the government saves be-

> Every dollar spent on SNAP benefits produces an additional $1.74 of economic activity during periods when the economy is weak.

tween $1.77 and $3.13 in future Medicaid costs on these infants and their mothers.[16] Another study by the nonpartisan Government Accountability Office reported that every dollar spent on WIC saved $2.89 in health care savings in the first year after birth and $3.50 over eighteen years.[17] Studies have also shown that 94% of Americans support this program.[18]

Tina from Yuba City, California, calls her two grown children "WIC graduates." She first walked into a WIC office when she was the young mother of a two-year-old son and pregnant with a little girl. She and her husband were not in poverty. But she was in college and her husband's work on a ranch did not pay enough for them to afford health insurance. WIC provided the nutrition and health care they needed for their two little children. The little boy got married last year and the curly haired little girl is now a junior in college. Tina herself graduated from college. "WIC was there for us when we needed it most," Tina says.[19]

But WIC is not a mandatory program. That means that people are not guaranteed WIC benefits even though they meet the eligibility requirements. In April 2011, in a deficit reduction deal between President Obama and Congress, $504 million was cut from this program. And the appropriations bill passed by the Republican-controlled House in June cut even more ($733 million). If that cut is enacted, more than 700,000 eligible poor women and children will probably be unable to benefit from WIC in 2012.[20]

Every dollar spent on WIC saved $2.89 in health care savings in the first year after birth and $3.50 over eighteen years.

Cutting programs like WIC and SNAP is not only morally wrong, it is economically silly. We know that preventative health care and nutritious food are among the best ways to avoid much more expensive future health care costs. Cutting WIC funding is an economically foolish way to reduce the deficit.

In addition to SNAP and WIC, the federal government has several other food assistance programs.[21] The largest is the National School Lunch Program that served nutritious lunches to 31 million lower-income children in 2009 and cost $9.8 billion.[22]

How does the amount of the federal government's food assistance to Americans compare to the food aid that comes from the tens of thousands of churches, nonprofit organizations and other private agencies that run soup kitchens and distribute food to needy people? The analysis varies a little. According to the widely respected Christian organization Bread for the World, all the food provided by all the private voluntary groups in the United States amounts to only 6% of the food aid provided to needy Americans by the federal government. So if we cut federal food aid by 6%, we wipe out the equivalent of all the private food assistance![23] Churches should do more, but they cannot begin to replace the food assistance provided by the federal government.

The Earned Income Tax Credit (EITC). The EITC is another example of a highly effective government program. In 2009 over 26 million people received about $59 billion from the EITC. That year, according to the IRS, the EITC lifted an estimated 6.6 million people out of poverty, including 3.3 million children.[24]

For every dollar of the first $12,780 earned in 2011 by a married low-income worker with two children, the family receives 40 cents as a tax credit. And if family income is so low that they owe no federal income taxes, they still receive the money as a tax refund. (That is what is meant by saying the EITC is a *refundable* tax credit). Up to a point the value of the tax credit increases with family size and earnings. Then as a family's income continues to increase beyond a certain point, the tax credit slowly phases out. The maximum amount of the EITC available to a family of four in 2011 was $5,160.[25]

The EITC has been a lifesaver for Anna, a single mother of six kids living in Colorado. She had to flee to another state to keep her kids and herself safe from an abusive husband. As a graduate student she only earned $17,000 a year—not enough for her and her six children. But the extra $4,300 from the EITC has helped her pay for school supplies, credit card bills and school loans. She will soon graduate with a master's degree in public administration with a focus on domestic violence. And she hopes to open a residential treatment facility for those convicted of domestic violence. She is making it, thanks to the EITC.[26]

Both Republicans and Democrats have supported the EITC. President Ronald Reagan, the first President Bush, President Clinton and President Obama have all increased it. The American Recovery and Reinvestment Act of 2009 expanded the EITC in two ways. It increased the benefit for families with three or more children (since these families are twice as likely to be poor as smaller families). And it reduced the marriage penalty, enabling married couples to receive larger benefits.[27]

Research demonstrates that the EITC is highly effective. It has encouraged single parents to get a job, reduced the welfare rolls and lifted millions out of poverty. It even moderates somewhat the gap between the rich and poor. During the last twenty-plus years, as we saw in chapter two, the share of national income going to the poorest 20% has declined while that received by the top 20% has grown dramatically. The EITC has offset from one-quarter to one-third of the drop in income to the bottom 20% of households with children.[28]

The EITC has one more wonderful benefit. It strengthens the family! Studies have shown that while the EITC increases workforce participation by single mothers, it *decreases* that by married mothers. That means that because of the EITC, more married mothers (or their husbands) can stay at home to provide good parenting for young children.[29] The EITC is pro-poor and pro-family.

The EITC lifts out of poverty more working families and more children than any other government program.[30] The success of the EITC is a decisive response to those who claim government programs never work.

Pell Grants. Pell Grants help college students from lower-income families go to college. In 2010–2011, the maximum Pell Grant was $5,550. In 2011–2012, Pell Grants helped 9.4 million college students at a cost of $35 billion.[31] More than 60% of students who received Pell Grants in 2009–2010 came from families with incomes less than $20,000—that is, families living about at or below the poverty level for a family of four.[32]

> The EITC has offset from one-quarter to one-third of the drop in income to the bottom 20% of households with children.

Students who receive Pell Grants are more likely to enroll in college full time. Only 40% of community college students enroll full time, but almost twice that share with Pell Grants do.

Unfortunately, the value of Pell Grants relative to the cost of attending a public four-year university has declined dramatically. Thirty years ago the Pell Grant covered three-quarters of those costs. Today, it is only one-third.[33]

The Pell Grant program is not free of problems. Some studies suggest that Pell Grants reduce dropout rates, especially for the neediest students.[34] But one by the U.S. Department of Education found no difference. Republican Congressman Ryan is right to say that "college graduation is the ultimate goal of the program."[35] A big part of the problem is high dropout rates for Pell Grant recipients at for-profit colleges and community colleges.[36] These problems are not caused by the Pell Grants, but they need to be corrected. We should demand that colleges provide academic tutoring and other reasonable supports to give students with Pell Grants every opportunity for success.

We should consider reducing the number of semesters that students may be eligible for Pell Grants. Currently, it is eighteen. Perhaps too we should tighten the requirements for satisfactory academic performance.[37]

Republicans have called for reducing the maximum grant from $5,500 to $3,000. Some Republican congressmen have even denounced Pell Grants as "welfare."[38] Unlike welfare, which can sometimes foster dependency, Pell Grants reward work. If a person does not work enough to get passing grades, he or she cannot continue. But if the student does work hard and receive a college degree, he or she is empowered for a lifetime—and pays taxes rather than collects welfare!

Congressman Ryan justified cuts in Pell Grants in order to reauthorize the D.C. Opportunity Scholarship Program—a voucher program that served poor and at-risk high school students in D.C. so they could attend private schools. (A Department of Education study has shown that this program significantly increased the probability of these students graduating from high school).[39] Congressman Ryan is right that President Obama and most Democrats have (wrongly, I believe) opposed experimenting with vouchers to see if they are an effective way to improve the educational success of low-income Americans. But we should not rob one good program to fund another. We urgently need vigorous new efforts to assure that a much higher percentage of poor and minority students graduate both from high school and college.

Cutting Pell Grants for college students from lower income families is not the way to solve our deficit crisis.

Head Start. At a cost of $7 billion a year, Head Start provides one million preschool children from poor homes with an educational experience designed to help them succeed in school. But in a provocative article in *Time* on July 7, 2011, Joe Klein claimed that Head Start "simply does not work." He cited a comprehensive impact study by the Department of Education that showed that there were few positive effects of the program. And even these modest good results disappeared by the end of first grade.[40]

Not all studies of Head Start have been this negative.[41] Some studies show that the program can have significant long-term impact, including higher graduation rates, lower arrest rates and better health. Research suggests that Head Start programs with better educated teachers, smaller classes and stronger supervision have better results.[42]

It is certainly obvious that an effective program with Head Start's goals is desperately needed. We all know that there are substantial numbers of young children in very poor homes that enter school with serious disadvantages. They simply never enjoyed a variety of experiences at home that would have enabled them to do well in school. We need a good, effective program for these children—even if it costs *more* than what we are currently spending on Head Start.

But if conclusive research shows that Head Start is not working well, then we must reform it or replace it with something that does. It makes no sense for people who care deeply about empowering poor neighbors to defend ineffective programs, even if they were designed with good intentions. We simply do not have enough resources to accept low standards or inefficiency. When there is a need to spend tax dollars on social programs like early education, then serious deficit reduction efforts demand that we hold these programs accountable for delivering the best results for our money.

DOMESTIC PROGRAMS EMPOWERING POOR NEIGHBORS

Programs	Necessary Action for Effectiveness
• SNAP (Food Stamps)	Fully fund
• WIC	Fully fund
• EITC	Keep
• Pell Grants	Correct weaknesses but do not cut
• Head Start	Evaluate thoroughly then improve or replace with effective alternative

Table 5.1.

The story of Angelique Melton shows the importance of effective federal antipoverty programs. In 2009, thanks to the economic downturn, she lost her $39,000 a year job at a construction firm. The only job she could find was a part-time position at Walmart paying $7,500. That put her (and her two children) well below the official poverty line of $17,400 for three. But Ms. Melton was now eligible for $3,600 a year in food stamps, $1,800 in nutritional supplements in the WIC program, plus about $4,000 in tax credits (largely the EITC). These government programs lifted Ms. Melton just to the poverty level. "They help you," she said. "I would not have made it otherwise."[43]

International economic foreign aid. Poll after poll over several decades has shown that a majority of Americans think that foreign aid to other countries takes about 25% of the total U.S. federal budget. And they want it cut. When asked what percent of the budget they think should go to foreign aid, they typically say 10%.[44] In fact, foreign economic aid is only about 1% of the federal budget.[45]

In FY2010, the total foreign assistance budget was $39.9 billion. But $14 billion of that was for military assistance or good governance programs (e.g., promoting democracy). About $21 billion was for food aid, refugees, disaster assistance, economic development, health and education.[46]

The United States currently spends about $2 billion per year on food aid. That $2 billion helps keep about 50 million people around the world from suffering or dying of malnutrition.[47]

In 2004, President Bush (thanks in significant part to his adviser and speech writer Michael Gerson) launched an ambitious new program called the President's Emergency Plan for AIDS Relief (PEPFAR). The goal was to treat 2 million people infected with AIDS. Later he expanded the program to treat malaria and tuberculosis, and increased the funding. In 2009, President Obama added still more funding. Since FY2001, U.S. foreign aid devoted to health care has jumped by 550%.[48]

In June 2011 the State Department reported that in FY2010 alone, PEPFAR treated 3.2 million people around the world with antiretroviral drugs that were saving their lives. The program also treated 800,000 HIV-positive mothers, enabling 114,000 babies to be born HIV-free. Through all of its programs (including those dealing with malaria and tuberculosis) the PEPFAR program directly provided health benefits to 11 million people, including about 3.8 million orphans, in thirty countries in FY2010. And it only cost about $6.9 billion.[49]

That represents phenomenal success! America is saving the lives of millions and improving the health of even more millions for just a few billion dollars a year.

That is not to claim that every dollar of our economic aid has been spent wisely. Here, as elsewhere, there are problems that need to be corrected.[50] But our PEPFAR and food aid programs represent phenomenal success. Literally saving millions of lives in poor countries is a highly effective pro-life agenda.

Sadly, in 2011 the Republican majority in the House chose to forsake President Bush's courageous leadership. They decided to dramatically cut the economic foreign aid budget.

Congressman Ryan's original proposal was a general cut of 29% in 2012 and 44% by 2016 of the total foreign affairs budget where economic foreign aid is located. In July, when the relevant committees in the Republican-controlled House made concrete decisions, we learned about the details. The House slashed 59% of the funds from the President's FY2012 request for multilateral assistance, 29% from his request for development assistance programs and 18% from global health (malaria, AIDS) programs. In virtually every case the funding proposed was substantially below what had been authorized for the previous year.[51]

Not surprisingly, Michael Gerson was furious. While Republicans in the House were talking about cutting the budget for crucial health programs in Africa, Gerson was in Senegal visiting new health programs made possible by American foreign aid. For centuries mosquitoes have spread malaria so effectively that millions of children regularly died. But if the mosquitoes land on a wall sprayed with insecticide or on a treated bed net, they die. Using money from President Bush's antimalaria program, Senegal set the target of universal bed-net coverage. Death by malaria dropped dramatically.

Gerson accused his fellow Republicans of abandoning programs started by President Bush. "If the goal of House Republicans is to squander the Republican legacy on global health, they are succeeding." Rightly he pointed out that "no one can reasonably claim that the budget crisis exists because America spends too much on bed nets and AIDS drugs."[52]

Gerson pointed out one last irony. Goree Island in Senegal was for three hundred years one of the main embarkation points for African slaves forced to travel to the New World. And right next to the stone opening to the Atlantic called the "door of no return" is a small cell where hundreds of enslaved children were stacked up in deadly conditions. Today, America is no longer killing Senegal's children, it is saving their lives. But will it continue?

Here as elsewhere Americans must make an historic choice. Is this the way we want to balance the budget?

A study by Citizens for Tax Justice revealed that from 2008 to 2010, 280 of the most profitable U.S. corporations, with total pretax profits of $1.4 trillion, received a total of nearly $224 billion in tax subsidies from the government.[53] More than half of these subsidies went to four industries: financial services, utilities, telecommunications and fuel (oil, gas and pipelines). Closing these subsidy loopholes would make up all of the cuts to food stamps planned by the Ryan budget, as well as covering the entire costs of WIC *and* foreign food aid, over the next ten years.[54] For the amount that taxpayers have given up to ultra-wealthy corporations in just three years, we could feed all of our most vulnerable families at home and millions more around the world for a decade.

FARM PROGRAMS

The funding for SNAP and other domestic food programs comes via the omnibus farm bill, which Congress will have to renew in 2012.[55] Significant parts of that bill should be changed. From 2005 to 2011, American taxpayers paid more than $30 billion to provide subsidies for corn-based ethanol. Most of those subsidies went to big oil companies to "encourage" them to use ethanol in gasoline even though they were already using ethanol and did not need subsidies to use it. Today, one-half of all U.S.-grown corn goes to produce ethanol—dramatically increasing global food costs. That seriously hurts poor people. There are other perfectly good substitutes for corn to produce ethanol, but corn-subsidized ethanol discourages research on these alternatives.[56] We should end this wasteful subsidy of ethanol.

In spite of this, Grover Norquist, head of Americans for Tax Reform, vigorously denounced Republican Senator Tom Coburn's call in the summer of 2011 to eliminate the special tax break on ethanol. Norquist's organization has been successfully pushing candidates for Congress to sign a "no tax increase" pledge since 1986. And Norquist claims that ending a misguided $30 billion tax break for big oil companies is a tax increase![57]

Another farm policy needing correction is the farm support paid primarily to farmers who grow corn, soybeans, wheat, cotton and rice. From 1995 to 2010 the United States spent $262 billion on these farm supports. Just the largest 10% of farms received 74% of the money. And the farmers got the payments both when the prices were high (when they did not need any subsidy) *and* when they were low (so they produced more than the market needed). And if that were not bad enough, these subsidies violate the rules of the World Trade Organization. And they hurt poor farmers in developing countries.[58] We should end almost all farm-support programs.

The savings from ending these two wasteful government subsidies could be used to reduce the federal deficit and expand effective programs reducing hunger here and abroad.

TAXES
Everybody would like to pay less in taxes. We would all like to keep more of our income rather than give it to the government.

At least a part of us feels that way. But we also know that if we want government to do anything, we must pay for that with our taxes. If we want government to operate fair courts, provide national security, support quality education for everyone, prevent hunger and starvation, empower poor people and help the elderly enjoy a decent life, we have to pay taxes.

In an important sense, paying taxes is one significant way we remember that God made us, not as isolated individuals, but as persons created for community. Taxes represent one substantial way we love our neighbors.

That does not mean every tax is wise. We must end duplicative, ineffective government programs. Furthermore, everybody agrees that the present tax code is a mess. It needs major change.

So what changes in the tax code would be wise and just and help us solve our deficit crisis?

It is essential to remember a few basic facts.

First, by comparison with other times and other countries, the taxes we pay today are low. As we saw in chapter two, the percent of income paid in taxes by all income levels has dropped in the last thirty years. The richest 1% saw the greatest drop, but everyone today pays a smaller percent of their income in taxes than three decades ago. And by comparison with other rich nations today, our taxes are very low. Many of the other rich nations today (members of the OECD) collect at least 10% more of their people's income in taxes than does the United States.

Taxes represent one substantial way we love our neighbors.

Second, overall, the American tax structure is only modestly progressive. Most people agree that the richer members of society should pay not only a larger dollar amount but also a larger percentage of their income in taxes. In fact, however, today's total tax code only modestly reflects that principle (see p. 38, table 2.2). Furthermore, progressivity has declined since 1960—in part because of tax cuts under President Reagan and the second President Bush that disproportionately benefited the richest Americans. The richest four hundred taxpayers saw their taxes fall from 30% of their income in 1995 to 16.6% in 2007. That saved these taxpayers $18 billion that year[59]— enough to fund the total WIC program for more than two years and almost enough to cover the total amount of the U.S. government's foreign aid for food aid, health care and economic development for a year.

Third, it is simply false to say that poorer Americans pay no taxes. Because of their low incomes, they owe no federal *income* taxes, but for every dollar they earn in wages, they pay 7.65 cents for the payroll tax that funds social security and Medicare. They also pay state and local sales taxes, which cost the poor a higher percent of their income than the rich. In 2010 the poorest 20%—with an average cash income of only $12,500—paid 16.2% of that on taxes (see p. 38, table 2.2).

Fourth, it is totally impossible to solve the deficit crisis solely by raising taxes. According to a study by the Congressional Research Service, if we had tried to eliminate the FY2011 deficit only by raising taxes, we would have had to increase the federal income tax by more than 140% or have raised both the federal income tax and the federal payroll tax by more than 70%.[60] Doing either would have sent the economy into a more severe recession and produced uncontrollable public anger and rebellion. What was true for 2011 is equally true for the longer term. We cannot solve the budget deficit only by raising taxes—or only by cutting expenditures.

Almost everyone agrees we need changes in the tax code. At the same time, there is certainly no widespread consensus on how to change it. Some want to cut taxes still more, claiming this will boost economic growth. Others, including Warren Buffett, think we should raise taxes somewhat, especially on the more wealthy. How should we decide?

I believe the following criteria for changing the federal tax code are grounded in both solid moral principles and economic analysis.

First, every working American should contribute something to help the nation solve the deficit crisis.

Second, overall, the tax code should be progressive. This means dealing with the fact that very rich people pay a much smaller percent of their income on the payroll tax than do most Americans. Furthermore, they also receive a great deal of income that is only taxed at the rate of 15% rather than the top income tax rate of 35%. Warren Buffett is right. We should "stop coddling the super-rich."[61]

Basic Facts

- American taxes are relatively low.
- Our tax structure is modestly progressive.
- The poor *do* pay taxes.
- The deficit crisis will not be solved solely by raising taxes.

Third, successful deficit reduction requires both cuts in federal expenditure and increases in taxes. Earlier, we saw that the Congressional Research Service has shown how impossible it would be to solve the deficit only by tax increases. But the same Congressional Research Service has also pointed out how difficult it would be to end the deficit solely with program cuts.

In 2010 that would have meant not spending a penny on national defense, education, infrastructure, foreign aid, research and much more.[62] Conservative evangelical leader Chuck Colson acknowledged the need for both with his pointed comment, "I see no biblical warrant for the two positions being embraced in Washington today—a total refusal to raise taxes on one hand; a total refusal to cut government spending on the other."[63] Colson is right.

It is politically significant that a solid majority of Americans agree that we need both budget cuts and tax increases. A CBS/New York Times poll on September 10-15, 2011, found that 71% agreed that the way to reduce the federal budget deficit was "a combination of both tax increases and spending cuts." Even 57% of Republicans agreed.[64]

Here are some of the specific changes we should make.

Capital gains and dividends. We should tax income from capital gains and dividends at the same rate as other income. (Capital gains refers to the difference in price between what one paid for something like a house or stock and the higher price received when it is sold; dividends are the income earned from things like stocks). Is there any reason why we should tax the income of a plumber, teacher or doctor at an upper rate of 35% and only tax income from capital gains and dividends at 15%? That is what happens today.

Criteria for Changing the Federal Tax Code

- Every working American should contribute something.
- The tax code should be progressive.
- We need both cuts in federal expenditure and increases in taxes.

And it is the reason megabillionaire Warren Buffett said in his famous piece in the *New York Times* that he paid income tax in

2010 at only a 17.4% rate while everyone else in his office had vastly less income but paid at an average rate of 36%.[65] This, Robert J. Samuelson says, is "the real tax avoidance scandal."[66] Is there any reason why twenty-five hedge-fund managers who made $25 billion in 2009 should only pay income taxes at a rate of 15% on that incredible income while people making vastly less money paid the top tax rate of 35%?[67]

In his FY2011 budget, President Obama proposed raising the rate on income from capital gains and dividends to 20% for high-income persons. But that is not good enough. It would leave the rate well below the 28% rate imposed under President Reagan.[68]

Some people argue that increasing the tax rate on income from capital gains and dividends to the rates that the rest of us pay on our income would discourage investment, hurt the economy and thus reduce job creation. Warren Buffett has a blunt response:

> I have worked with investors for 60 years and I have yet to see anyone—not even when capital gains rates were 39.9 percent in 1976-77—shy away from a sensible investment because of the tax rate on the potential gain. People invest to make money and potential taxes have never scared them off. And to those who argue that higher rates hurt job creation, I would note that a net of nearly 40 million jobs were added between 1980 and 2000. You know what's happened since then: lower tax rates and far lower job creation.[69]

Income tax. Federal income tax rates have varied greatly over the last century. The income tax has always been progressive because there have always been a number of brackets with increasingly higher marginal tax rates. Lower-income people fall into a bracket that taxes most or all their income at a lower percent. As income increases, more of a person's income falls into a higher tax bracket that imposes income tax at a higher percent. The marginal tax rate is the percent that an individual pays on the last dollar earned.

Both the top marginal tax rate and the number of brackets have changed dramatically. At some periods there have been well over a dozen brackets. Today we have six: 10%, 15%, 25%, 28%, 33% and 35%. At one point the top income tax rate was 91%. During almost all the time of the great economic growth from 1950 to 1980, the top bracket was 50% or more.

The National Commission on Fiscal Responsibility and Reform (Simpson-Bowles) appointed by President Obama recommended reducing the tax brackets to only three: 12%, 22% and 28%.[70] But that would mean both increasing the percent of taxable income paid by the least wealthy taxpayers and lowering the percent for the richest. Unless other adjustments were made, that would contradict their own principle to "maintain or increase progressivity in the tax code."[71]

I believe we should keep the current six brackets and add one or two more. Under the present system of six brackets, people with incomes of $350,001 pay the same top marginal income tax rate as taxpayers with incomes of $10 million or $100 million. There is no reason why people with incomes over one million cannot pay at a top marginal tax rate of 40% to 45%. For those with income over $5 million, the top marginal rate could be 50%.

Some argue that raising taxes on the wealthy is futile because the additional revenues won't come close to making up our deficit. In 2009 the United States had 236,833 millionaires, with a total adjusted gross income of about $727 billion. Taxing this group at a 10% higher rate would generate at most $73 billion in new revenue. This comes to only 2% of federal spending.[72] This does not sound like much. Yet it is completely misleading to discount $73 billion as negligible, while at the same time claiming that we cannot afford to maintain our current level of foreign humanitarian assistance, which comes to less than a third of this amount (about $21 billion), or that fiscal responsibility demands trimming Pell Grants, which serve over 9 million students at half of this amount ($35 billion). If every bit counts, then we can't afford tax cuts. If tax cuts don't matter to the deficit, then neither do important social investments such as food assistance and access to college.

Some, again, may argue that increasing the taxes paid by the wealthy would hurt the economy. But careful analysis shows that annual growth in GDP was higher in the years when the top marginal tax rate was above 60% than in later years when it was below 40%.[73]

Some conservatives and liberals have suggested that we should change the income tax code by reducing or ending what the economists call "tax expenditures."[74] Tax expenditures are deductions (e.g., for charitable donations), exemptions and tax credits that lower the amount of income tax owed. In FY2010 these tax expenditures added up to about $1 trillion—that is more than the total individual income tax ($898.5 billion) collected that year.[75] Ending a large portion of these tax expenditures would increase federal revenues—unless, as many Republicans propose, we cut the income tax rates by comparable amounts.

But before we hastily end all tax expenditures we need to carefully examine the merit of each. The second largest one is the deduction for interest paid on one's house mortgage.[76] This deduction should be reduced so it covers only one house and only the first $300,000 or $400,000 on the mortgage. Currently, a person can deduct mortgage interest even on a vacation home. In 2011 that cost the U.S. Treasury $800 million![77] That is more than enough to cover the cuts to housing programs for the elderly and disabled proposed by the House Budget Committee Chairman. But the mortgage deduction should not be eliminated entirely because encouraging Americans to own their own home nurtures family stability. Nor should we cut or end the Earned Income Tax Credit, which strengthens low-income workers, or the Child Tax Credit, which strengthens the family.[78]

The deduction for charitable contributions is also too important to lose. President Obama has wrongly proposed reducing this deduction for high-income people. I think we should retain this deduction because it encourages donations to a wide variety of nonprofit organizations—churches, orchestras, ministries serving the poor—which contribute greatly to society.[79]

Some of these tax expenditures should be eliminated. But a number of them, as the Simpson-Bowles Commission recommended, should be kept.[80]

One other change in the federal income tax would, I believe, be significant. One of the criteria I have already stated is that everyone contribute. I believe that it would be good for American society if we could develop a widespread understanding that everyone can and should contribute to the common good by helping to avoid a crisis that would hurt everyone.

We could add a surtax to the income tax in a way that every person who files a federal income tax form would contribute something. For low-income folk who owe no income tax or receive a refundable tax credit, the amount should be very modest; no more than $25 or $50. Anyone who owes federal income tax would pay a surcharge on what they owe. The surcharge could start at 1% of the income tax owed and scale up to 10% for people who owe more than $10,000. Every taxpayer—not just the millionaires, not just those who earn more than $250,000—should contribute.

Once the budget is balanced, the surtax would be abolished. If the budget fell into deficit again for three consecutive years, the surtax would return after the economy had recovered.

During the Second World War, there was a widespread feeling in America that everyone was working together, sacrificing for the common good. We need to recover that spirit to solve our deficit crisis. This kind of surtax could help develop a widespread commitment to working together for the benefit of all.

Payroll tax. The social security payroll tax, as we have seen, falls disproportionately on the less wealthy for three reasons. First, it is not progressive since the rate (6.2% for employees) is the same regardless of income.[81] Second, only the first $106,800 of wages are subject to the social security payroll tax, so people with very high incomes pay only a very small proportion of their income in this tax. Finally, capital gains and dividends are not subject to the payroll tax at all.

We need changes here, but I will discuss those in the section on social security.

Estate tax. The estate tax is levied on inherited property when it is passed on to heirs after a person's death. This tax (called a "death tax" by many Republicans) was gradually reduced by President George W. Bush. It was fully phased out in 2010. But it returned in 2011 with a much higher exemption ($5 million) and an historically low rate.[82]

Very wealthy people like Warren Buffett and Bill Gates's father believe we should keep the estate tax. Bill Gates Sr. points out that every highly successful businessperson succeeds in part because of the many benefits (e.g., educated employees, legal systems, public safety systems, good transportation systems) provided by the larger society through government. Taxes like the estate tax are a kind of repayment: "a payback to society, the price of building and protecting wealth in the

United States."[83] Warren Buffett told Pulitzer Prize–winning
reporter David Cay Johnston that repealing the estate tax
"would be a terrible mistake" comparable to "choosing the 2020
Olympic team by picking the eldest sons of the gold-medal
winners in the 2000 Olympics." "We have come closer to a true
meritocracy than anywhere else around the world," Buffett continued. "You have mobility, so people with talents can be put to
the best use. Without the estate tax, you in effect will have an
aristocracy of wealth, which means you pass down the ability
to command the resources of the nation based on heredity
rather than merit."[84] Surely one of the richest men in the world
cannot be accused of "class warfare" when he advocates for re-
taining or increasing taxes on the very rich.

No estate tax is charged on the part of an estate that goes to
charitable organizations. Consequently this tax encourages
charitable donations that strengthen civil society.

I would support an estate tax of 40% with an exemption of
$2-$4 million (and up to $6 million for family farms and small
family businesses). For estates above $50 million, the rate could
be at least 50%. We should also close many of the loopholes
that wealthy people currently use to reduce this tax.

Carbon tax. The scientific evidence has become increasingly
clear that the vast amounts of carbon dioxide released into the
atmosphere because of our burning of fossil fuels is creating
climate change that will have very bad, probably devastating,
consequences.[85] One major proposal to reduce the use of fossil
fuels and make renewable energy more competitive is to put a
tax on carbon dioxide emissions. A carbon tax could easily
raise $100 billion a year.[86]

A major problem with a carbon tax is that it is regressive—it
falls most heavily on the poor. Therefore, if a carbon tax were
adopted, that portion of the income raised that is needed to

offset its impact on low-income people should go for that purpose. The rest could be used to reduce the deficit. That would be good both for the budget and the global ecosystem. It would also contribute to intergenerational justice since our grandchildren will suffer from or rejoice in the world we leave them. Our current desire for cheap energy is creating a world full of huge problems for future generations.

Financial transactions tax. The volume of financial transactions has exploded in recent years. Many are appropriate and helpful, but some are highly speculative and are harmful to the economy. A very small tax on financial transactions (e.g., stock purchases) would discourage harmful speculation and raise significant revenue. Both Hong Kong and Singapore impose such taxes—and Hong Kong and Singapore score at the top of the very conservative Heritage Foundation's Index of Economic Freedom.[87]

CHANGES IN THE TAX CODE

AREAS OF PROPOSED CHANGE	SUGGESTED CHANGES
Tax on capital gains and dividends	• same rate as all other income

Income tax	• keep current six brackets
	• add two more brackets
	  $1 million+ 40-45%
	  $5 million+ 50%
	• keep good deductions
	• add deficit reduction surcharge so every tax filer contributes

Estate tax	• 40% after exemption • 50% on estates above $50 million
Carbon tax	• enact with offset for lower-income people
Financial transactions tax	• enact a very small tax on each transaction

Table 5.2.

The tax changes discussed here do not by any means cover all possibilities.[88] But if implemented they would substantially reduce the federal deficit, make the tax code more progressive, modestly reduce income inequality and provide significant income to fund important, effective federal programs.

We must, however, deal with one major objection. Many conservatives argue that increasing taxes on the wealthy is exactly the wrong thing to do. Everybody agrees that creating more jobs and thus boosting the economy is the best way to solve the deficit crisis. And a key argument of Republican Congressman Ryan and other conservative economic proposals is that the best way to create jobs is to cut taxes—especially for those in the highest tax brackets, whom Ryan calls "the most successful job creators in America."[89] There are several problems with this argument.

First, we have little evidence that cutting taxes for the wealthy inevitably spurs job creation. In fact, recent history suggests the opposite. The tax cuts enacted by President George W. Bush did generate some employment growth, but it was only about 1% a year—slower than any decade since 1940.[90] During his eight years in office, net employment rose by about 3 million jobs. In contrast, despite an increase in the top income tax rate, President Clinton's tenure in office saw the net creation of 23 million jobs.[91]

Second, the economic model used to predict a positive economic impact from tax cuts has a seriously flawed track record. Ryan and others have relied on the same team of economists from The Heritage Foundation who advocated the original set of Bush tax cuts. In 2001 these analysts forecasted that "the Bush plan would significantly increase economic growth and family income while substantially reducing the federal debt."[92]

The actual results were quite different. The economic model used by Heritage analysts significantly overestimated GDP growth rates and other economic indicators.[93] The Bush tax cuts did result in significantly higher taxable income in the four years before the 2007 recession[94]—but as I noted earlier, this was largely due to a rapid growth of income for the wealthy and not from substantial growth in income for most people.[95] Median household income actually fell 0.6% from 2000 to 2007.[96] And federal debt increased by nearly $5 trillion, with half of that attributable to the tax cuts.[97] The inconsistencies in the model have led a number of economists to question the Ryan plan's rosy economic projections.[98]

Third, this model cannot explain our current high levels of unemployment. The Heritage analysis of the Ryan budget predicts, "Lower taxes stimulate greater investment, which expands the size of business activity. This expansion fuels a demand for more labor, which enters a labor market that contains workers who themselves face lower taxes. Consequently, significantly higher employment ensues."[99] If this were true, then why do we face historically high levels of unemployment, since capital gains taxes are at historic lows, total taxes taken in by the federal government are at their lowest level since 1950, taxpayers at all income levels enjoy lower rates, and the greatest cuts in effective tax rates over the past ten years have gone to the wealthiest households, said to be the "job creators"?[100]

Nor can all our economic problems be blamed on burdensome regulations. The total average annual direct cost to businesses of all regulations under President Obama is estimated between $7 and $11 billion—at most, less than one-tenth of a percent of the total economy.[101] In fact, many believe that the recession was partly caused by a lack of wise financial regulations.[102] Clearly, lowering taxes and reducing government are not sufficient to counter the effects of the recession and restore economic growth.

Fourth, this model argues that tax cuts to the wealthy are

necessary because it assumes that this group is responsible for producing value and creating jobs, whether directly as business owners or indirectly as consumers and investors. Yet some in the top tax brackets make their money by *eliminating* American jobs—whether by outsourcing jobs overseas or by slashing their payrolls to improve their bottom line. Others gained their huge wealth not by adding to the economy but through shady financial practices that helped bring on the recession.[103] Most small business owners—considered the engine of job growth— do not fall into the top income brackets.[104]

Finally, research indicates that cutting taxes is not the most cost-efficient way to promote economic growth. A study by Moody's Analytics estimates that making the Bush tax cuts permanent would return only 35 cents in economic activity for every dollar in revenue lost. But every dollar spent on the Earned Income Tax Credit generates $1.24 in economic activity, and spending on infrastructure returns $1.44.[105] A Congressional Budget Office study ranked various policy options by numbers of jobs created per million dollars spent. Extending unemployment benefits and reducing payroll taxes were the top job creators. The policy that came in last? Reducing income taxes.[106]

Creating jobs is vital to restoring our nation's fiscal health. We cannot find long-term solutions to our debt crisis without sustained economic growth. But the argument that the only or best way to create jobs is to cut taxes is based on flawed, simplistic economic analysis.

Raising taxes is one essential part of a balanced solution to the budget crisis. But so is cutting expenditures. This becomes especially clear when we look at the three huge areas of social security, health programs and defense. As figure 5.1 shows, in 2010 well over half of the federal budget—$2.185

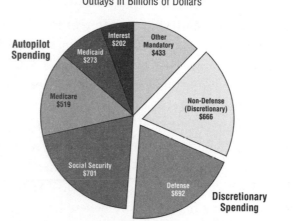

TOTAL SPENDING IN FY2010 = $3.5 TRILLION
Outlays in Billions of Dollars

Figure 5.1. Source: Congressional Budget Office August 2010 Budget & Economic Outlook. Figure displayed in *Concurrent Resolution on the Budget—Fiscal Year 2012*, Report of the Committee on the Budget, House of Representatives, "The Path to Prosperity: Restoring America's Promise," April 5, 2011, pp. 5-6.

trillion or 62%—went to these three areas.[107] We simply must find savings in all these areas—no matter how hard that will be politically.

SOCIAL SECURITY

Social security is the most successful antipoverty program in American history. Seniors used to suffer from the highest level of poverty in the country. Today the elderly enjoy the lowest poverty rates. Less than 10% (9.7%) of our seniors were in poverty in 2008. But if we had not had social security, almost half (45.2%) of all seniors would have been in poverty that year.[108]

It is essential to understand what social security is and is not. It is not an individual retirement investment program where workers personally invest money and receive in retirement exactly what they invested plus earnings. Rather, social security is a social insurance program designed to guarantee that all workers and their spouses have at least a modestly adequate income as seniors. But it is also a kind of life insurance plan because it provides payments to spouses and children of workers who die young. Furthermore, it is also a disability insurance giving a modest income to disabled workers. We pay for it through the payroll tax of 12.4% of our wages. One half is paid by the worker and one half by the employer.

In 2010, 53.4 million Americans received social security. Three-quarters (41 million) were seniors. But 2.3 million were children of workers who had died. Ten million were disabled workers.[109]

Social security has many positive benefits.

It is our most successful antipoverty program. In 2008 it lifted almost 20 million Americans out of poverty. Over 13 million were seniors, but over 1 million were children and over 5 million were disabled workers.

Its benefits are highly progressive. Since the benefits received as a senior are partly dependent on what one paid in payroll taxes, people who earned more and therefore paid more in payroll taxes receive higher social security benefits.[110] But the program is designed to especially benefit poorer workers. As figure 5.2 shows, lower-income people receive a much higher percent of their average wage in retirement benefits than do the highest paid workers.

Social security benefits women for several reasons. Even if they never worked outside the home (and never paid any payroll taxes), married women receive one-half of their husband's social security benefits and 100% when he dies. Women live longer than men and therefore collect more benefits. Women pay only 40% of payroll taxes but collect 49% of social security benefits. It is also especially important for African Americans and Hispanics.[111]

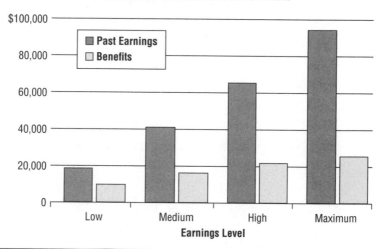

Figure 5.2. Source: Social Security Administration, 2010 Trustees Report. CBPP, "Policy Basics," p. 2.

Social security benefits for seniors are really quite modest—
on *average*, only $1,170 a month or about $14,000 a year in
2010.[112] But that modest income provided the majority of all
their income for 55% of all seniors. And it provided over 90%
for one-quarter of our elderly folk.[113]

But the social security program has a major problem that
must be solved. It is primarily a "pay-as-you-go" system. Current
payroll taxes of current workers pay for the checks that go to
retired workers. As figure 5.3 shows, in 1960 there were 5.1
workers paying the payroll tax for every beneficiary. Today it is
about 3.0 and by 2040 it will be about 2.1. The baby-boom generation is starting to retire in large numbers, creating a much
larger number of retirees collecting social security. We are
living longer so we will collect benefits longer. Workers today
retire younger than they used to. And, as we saw earlier, high
wage earners only pay the payroll tax on the first $106,800;

therefore a smaller percentage of the nation's total income is now subject to the payroll tax than earlier.[114]

For years the payroll tax raised more money than was needed to pay that year's social security benefits. But in 2010 the payroll tax provided less income than was needed for that year's benefits.[115] And that gap will grow larger year by year. For the many years when the payroll tax collected more than was needed for

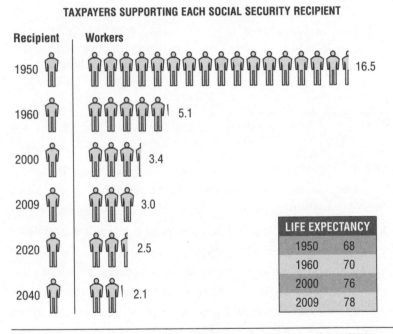

TAXPAYERS SUPPORTING EACH SOCIAL SECURITY RECIPIENT

Recipient	Workers	
1950		16.5
1960		5.1
2000		3.4
2009		3.0
2020		2.5
2040		2.1

LIFE EXPECTANCY	
1950	68
1960	70
2000	76
2009	78

Figure 5.3. Source: 2010 Annual Report of the Board of Trustees of the Federal Old-Age and Survivors Insurance and Federal Disability Insurance Trust Funds, p. 53.

the year's benefits, the balance was invested in the Social Security Trust. But the federal government simply borrowed that balance and spent it on other things that year. The Social Security Trust Fund has about $2.6 trillion that can pay full benefits until about 2037 without any changes.[116] But that $2.6

trillion is not invested in some nongovernmental agency that can now be required to provide those funds as needed. Since the government spent that $2.6 trillion it borrowed from the Trust Fund years ago, the only way the government can pay back the Trust Fund is by raising taxes, cutting some other expenditures or borrowing more money and adding to the debt.

There is no instant crisis. There is no disaster lurking in three or six years. Nor is the problem insurmountable. But there is a problem that dare not be ignored. In about 2037 the Social Security Trust Fund will be exhausted. After that, income from the social security payroll tax will only be enough to pay 75% of promised benefits. The longer we wait to fix it, the harder it will be. The longer we wait, the more drastic will be the necessary tax increases or benefit cuts.

As we decide how to fix social security, we need to remember our basic principles. We love our neighbors, respect their God-given dignity and implement God's special concern for the poor as we seek to guarantee the material well-being of seniors. We also implement our belief that God created us for community as we promote the common good across economic classes and the generations. Social security is a way that almost everyone shares in the cost of guaranteeing to all workers both disability insurance and a modest retirement income.

We dare not forget the issue of intergenerational justice. Children have an obligation to care for their parents and grandparents, but seniors also have an obligation not to demand excessive benefits now at the expense of their children and grandchildren.

The poverty rate for children is higher than it is for seniors![117] Part of the reason is that seniors vote and children do not. So the government is more likely to provide benefits to seniors than quality education for children. As Fareed Zakaria noted in a 2011 column in *Time*, "the federal government spends $4 on every adult over 65, compared with $1 on every child under 18. That is a statement about our priorities, favoring consumption over investment, the present over the future, ourselves over our children."[118]

We need courageous seniors who are willing to promote changes that will cost them money in order to promote intergenerational justice.

So what should we do?

We need to gradually increase money collected in taxes and slowly reduce benefits. A 50-50 split seems wise.

We can increase income in several ways.

Today, only a portion of social security income is subject to the federal income tax. No matter how much other income seniors have, some of their social security benefits are tax free![119] In 2008 a quarter of all families headed by a person 65 or older enjoyed incomes over $75,000.[120] But they still paid no income tax on some of their social security income. For persons and couples with combined income (social security benefits and other income) over 200% of the poverty level, the amount of social security benefits subject to the federal income tax should increase. Above 300-400% of the poverty level, all social security income should be subject to the federal income tax. Seniors who advocate for that change will be taking a courageous stand for intergenerational justice.

Second, we should end the current practice in which the richest people with the highest incomes pay no payroll tax at all on a great deal of their income. No matter how many millions a person makes in income, he or she pays the social security payroll tax only on the first $106,800. Because the richest Americans have in recent decades received a higher percent of total income, the amount of total income in the economy subject to the payroll tax has actually dropped from

91% in 1983 to 83% in 2009.[121] That should change. The national commission led by Simpson and Bowles recommended that we slowly increase that amount to $190,000 by 2050.[122] I think we should move much faster, increasing it to that amount no later than 2021. In addition, the richest Americans should pay some social security payroll tax (no less than 3%) on all income above $190,000.

Third, investment income (income from dividends and capital gains) is not subject to the payroll tax. Over ten years we should progressively apply the employee's share (6.2%) of the payroll tax to investment income.

We also need to trim benefits.

Since people are more healthy and live longer, it is reasonable to expect them to work a little longer. Under current law the retirement age (for full benefits) will be 67 in 2027. Simpson-Bowles recommended gradually raising the full retirement age to 68 by 2050 and 69 by 2075 and increasing the early retirement age (in lockstep) to 63 and 64.[123] That seems wise.

There is an important objection to this. Workers who do heavy manual labor may not be able to work to 68 or 69. But we can deal with that problem by using that part of the social security program that provides disability benefits to workers no longer able to work.

Second, we should use a more accurate annual cost of living adjustment. The technical details are not important here. But the current annual increase in social security benefits actually is slightly higher than an accurate calculation of the true increase in the cost of living for the population as a whole.[124] Seniors should take the lead in requesting this change.

Third, we should slowly reduce the benefits for the richest one-quarter of social security beneficiaries.[125]

In addition to raising additional income and reducing some

benefits, we should increase social security benefits for the poorest retirees. Currently, social security has a special minimum benefit to help the poorest, but it is not adequate. We should increase the special minimum benefit for the poorest to at least 133% of the federal poverty level for retirees with at least thirty years of creditable work. We also need a modest increase in benefits for the very elderly who often outlive their savings.[126]

Finally, we need a reasonable increase in Supplemental Security Income (SSI), which helps the disabled and the very poor elderly regardless of prior work. Current benefits do not even lift those people to the poverty level. They should.

Here, as always, we must act decisively against fraud. On occasion, those administering disability benefits (SSI) have granted them carelessly or even dishonestly to people who are not truly disabled.[127] Such actions rightly anger citizens and undermine support for those who truly need disability benefits.[128]

Some (including President George W. Bush) have argued that the way to solve social security's problems is to privatize it. We should cut or end the payroll tax and let individuals invest the money saved in private pension funds. But that is problematic for several reasons. First, the cost of transition would be huge since we would have to both continue social security benefits to present retirees who did not have this money to invest in private pension funds while at the same time dramatically reducing the amount of current income from the payroll tax.

Second, a worker would have no guarantee of a minimum income from the private pension fund. If the stock market collapsed as a person was retiring, his or her income for retirement could quickly drop dramatically.

Third, the single social security system we now have is cheaper to administer than hundreds of different private plans. Administrative costs for social security are less than 1% (only .9%) of annual benefits—far below that of private retirement annuities.[129]

Finally, the present social security system is pro-poor and pro-family. Lower-income workers receive a much higher percent of what they earned as workers than do higher income folk. And the current system provides, as we saw earlier, major benefits to a spouse (usually the wife) who earned less or nothing because s/he stayed home to care for the children. A wife receives 50% of her husband's benefits even if she never worked outside the home. All these pro-poor, pro-family benefits would disappear in a privatized system. That is why Christian conservative leader Gary Bauer (president of the Family Research Council until he ran for U.S. president) vigorously opposed privatizing social security in a widely discussed op-ed in the *New York Times*.[130]

SAVING SOCIAL SECURITY

1. Increase income
- tax more of the social security income of higher income seniors
- quickly increase amount of income subject to payroll tax
- apply payroll tax to investment income

2. Lower costs
- slowly increase retirement age for full benefits
- adopt more accurate cost of living adjustment
- slowly reduce benefits to richest 1/4 of social security recipients

3. Strengthen the poorest
- increase minimum benefit for poorest to at least 133% of poverty level
- increase Supplemental Security Income to poverty level

4. Do not privatize

Table 5.3.

Social security is a highly successful government program. It must—and can—be fixed, not dismantled. Seniors can lead the way as they champion justice both for poorer seniors now and for their children and grandchildren in the future.

HEALTH CARE

It is generally agreed that rapidly rising health care costs pose our biggest fiscal challenge. They are the primary drivers of long-term federal budget deficits.[131] Fixing this problem will be exceedingly difficult.

The federal government has three major health care programs: Medicare, Medicaid and CHIP (or SCHIP).

Medicare provides health care (paying for much of the cost of doctors, medication and hospitalization) for almost all seniors and for a much smaller number of persons with disabilities. In 2010, Medicare covered about 47 million Americans at a cost to the federal government of $519 billion.[132]

Medicaid is a means-tested program that provides health care to poor Americans. The eligibility requirements vary somewhat for different people but Medicaid typically provides coverage (or will by 2014) for people who are not elderly with incomes below 133% of the poverty level. The majority is not seniors, but a substantial amount of the total cost pays for long-term nursing care for seniors who run out of money. In 2010 the cost to the federal government was about $273 billion. Since the costs are shared with the states, state governments added more than $100 billion for this program.[133]

Finally, the State Children's Health Insurance Program (SCHIP)—often called CHIP—is a joint federal/state program that provides health insurance for children in families with incomes too high to be eligible for Medicaid but too low to be able to purchase private insurance. Started in 1997 and expanded to cover four million more children in 2009, it covered 7.7 million children in 2010.

These programs contribute enormously to the well-being of Americans. Before Medicare was started in 1965, more than half (51%) of all seniors lacked health insurance. Today almost all seniors sign up for Medicare. There are significant co-pays, but the vast majority of seniors can be confident that they can afford quality health care.

For some time some health economists and policymakers have questioned whether Medicaid truly improves the lives of the poor. Then in 2008 an unusual situation in Oregon provided an opportunity for the kind of randomized study that is considered the gold standard by researchers. The state wanted to expand Medicaid coverage, but it only had money to cover 10,000 people, and 90,000 applied. So Oregon decided to randomly select 10,000. That meant that health economists at Harvard and MIT could compare what happened to those who received Medicaid with those who did not. The result, published in 2011, was the first rigorously controlled evaluation of the impact of Medicaid.

The results were impressive. Those covered by Medicaid were 35% more likely to go to a clinic or see a doctor, and 30% more likely to be admitted to a hospital. Women with Medicaid were 60% more likely to have mammograms. People with Medicaid were 70% more likely to go to a specific clinic or office for medical care, and 50% more likely to have a personal doctor they usually saw. Compared with those without insurance, those with Medicaid were 40% less likely to say their health had gotten worse, and 25% more likely to say their health was good or excellent. Medicaid clearly has very positive effects.[134]

But there is a problem with federal health care programs, especially Medicare. Figure 5.4, which comes from Congressman Ryan's budget proposals (using Congressional Budget Office data), shows that, unless there are changes, by about 2050, the cost of social security and health care would consume every dollar collected in federal taxes! Even after we note that Ryan's income projections are very low, since he assumes no tax increases (in fact more tax cuts), it is still clear that we have a huge problem. A study by the Congressional Research Service noted that Medicare spending increased 8% per year for the past twenty years. Even with the projected savings under President Obama's health care bill, it is expected to continue to rise

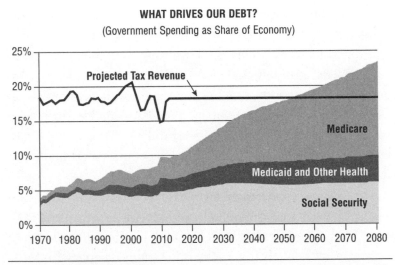

WHAT DRIVES OUR DEBT?
(Government Spending as Share of Economy)

Figure 5.4. Source: CBO. *Concurrent Resolution on the Budget—Fiscal Year 2012,* Report of the Committee on the Budget, House of Representatives, "The Path to Prosperity: Restoring America's Promise," April 5, 2011, p. 16.

by 6% a year.[135] The Medicare trustees reported in 2008 that Medicare costs were expected to jump from 3.1% of GDP in 2006 to 7% in 2035 and 10.7% in 2080.[136]

The reasons for this rapid growth in Medicare costs are several. General health care costs in America are rising much faster than the GDP because of expensive advances in health care delivery and medical technology, longer life spans and a growing percentage of the population over sixty-five (older people have higher medical costs). Medicare is affected by all these problems plus the fact that in 2011 the baby-boomer generation started to turn sixty-five—and thus became eligible for Medicare.[137]

The Centers for Medicare and Medicaid Services report that the shortfall in income for Medicare's hospital insurance would be much worse without President Obama's 2010 Affordable Care Act.[138] But it is still in trouble.

It is important to realize that the financial problems of Medicare are not unique to federal health care programs. The costs of government health care programs are not rising any faster than health care offered by private insurers. Private health insurance companies jumped their rates by about 9% in 2011. The Congressional Budget Office predicted that without significant changes, total American spending on health care would rise from 16% of GDP in 2007 to 25% in 2025, 37% in 2050 and 49% in 2082.[139] Spending one-third or one-half of all our GDP on health care is simply impossible. There must be fundamental changes in our entire health care system, not just in federal programs.

Other countries with equally good or better results for their people spend a far smaller amount per person on health care than we do. In fact, the United States spends about twice as much per person on health care as do fifteen other rich nations (including Germany, Canada, Japan, France, UK, Sweden) in the Organization for Economic Co-operation and Development.[140]

So what should we do? Some argue that the best solution is a government-run, single-payer system like that in Canada. Most Canadians like the system, but it has problems, including substantial waiting time for nonurgent procedures. Politically, it seems impossible even to test such a model, much less adopt it in the United States.

There are other models. Switzerland has a system that covers everyone using private insurers. The private insurance companies must cover everyone and everyone must buy insurance. The government provides subsidies for lower-income people. The Swiss enjoy a longer life expectancy than Americans even though they spend far less of their GDP on health care.[141]

Without adopting a fundamentally different model, Americans could realize significant savings with several important changes.

We should almost certainly move away from our current fee-for-service approach. That rewards doctors and hospitals for the number of office visits, expensive tests and procedures they perform, not for their success in preventive care. If they spend time designing effective preventive care, they lose money—both because designing new strategies takes time and because they have fewer office visits and hospitalizations to bill. President Obama's Affordable Care Act (2010) has a number of pilot programs to move toward preventive care. We need to move much further toward paying doctors and hospitals primarily "on the number of patients cared for and the quality of that care," rather than on the number of tests, office visits and operations they order.[142]

Programs to reduce growing obesity would reduce long-term health care costs. If current trends continue, by 2020 obesity and overweight will account for one-fifth of all health care expenses.[143] If we simply imposed a tax of one cent per ounce on sugar-sweetened drinks, we would help reduce obesity and raise $79 billion over six years.[144] Also, as we saw earlier, reforming medical malpractice law to limit the amount of awards for noneconomic and punitive damages would also help.

We also need to face the implications of an important medical statistic. On average, about 27%-30% of all Medicare costs are incurred during the last year of life.[145] Since almost all seniors receive Medicare, it is reasonable to say that about 27%-30% of all medical costs for seniors are incurred in the last year of their life.

One cause of this large medical expense in the last twelve months of a person's life is that both the medical profession and Americans generally choose to take extraordinary measures that are enormously expensive to prolong life even when the best medical wisdom is that death is almost inevitable within a few weeks or months. A recent study of all operations on Medicare participants in the last year of their life discovered that in 2008, about one out of three had surgery during their last year. One out of five had surgery in the last month and one out of ten in the last week![146] That is not to suggest that none of those operations should have happened. Frequently doctors simply do not know whether an operation will lead to renewed health and significantly prolonged life. But too often doctors operate to fix something they know they can correct even though they also know some other more basic problem (which they cannot fix) is leading to inevitable death.[147]

Performing useless operations or engaging in other extraordinary measures when death is inevitable in a few weeks or months is wrong. Survey after survey has shown that seniors do not want that.[148] And it is not just economically foolish, it is morally wrong and theologically misguided. And there is a very good way to help correct this problem. It is called a "living will" or an "advanced directive."

I have one, and it explains that if my mind and body are irreversibly damaged so that death is near, I do not want expensive, extraordinary measures to be taken to prolong my life for a brief period. It says, "The approach that I favor is one of aggressive treatment for potentially reversible illness, but predominately comfort care for progressive and irreversible disease."

That, I believe, is a solidly pro-life approach. For decades, I have championed a conservative agenda on pro-life issues.[149] I am strongly opposed to abortion and euthanasia. I vigorously oppose any suggestion that we should legalize euthanasia.

But there is a huge difference between taking active steps to intentionally kill a person on the one hand and not taking extraordinary measures to prolong life for a few weeks or months when the best medical wisdom is that death is near because the disease is irreversible. The first is always wrong. The second is good and wise. If and when I face almost certain death, I do not want to be in a hospital entangled in multiple tubes and elaborate gadgets. I want to be at home with my family. I want to be as comfortable as possible as my children and grandchildren surround me rereading the great biblical promises about the resurrection and singing songs in which they promise to meet me on the other side.

We should encourage everyone to write a living will.

Fighting, at enormous cost, to stay alive a few more weeks when death is near and inevitable irresponsibly adds significant economic costs for younger folk.[150] That is morally wrong. And it smacks of religious doubt. Do we not truly believe that death is a transition to a glorious future in the presence of the risen Lord?

It is time for evangelical Christians who are strongly pro-life to take a clear public stand on this issue. We must insist on the huge distinction between intentionally taking steps to kill a person and simply letting irreversible disease run its course.

We should encourage everyone to write a living will that embraces that distinction.

We should also vigorously and loudly object to political demagogues who denounce any attempt to encourage people to prepare living wills. To shout about "death panels," as some did in 2010, when a proposal in federal health care legislation was designed to pay for a conversation between a patient and his or her doctor about a living will was irresponsible and dishonest.

Of course there are dangers. There are people who champion legalizing euthanasia. There will be people who for narrow economic reasons do not want to pay for health care for the disabled and the elderly. We must work hard to respect the sanctity of human life from conception to natural death. But that does not mean we ought to spend large amounts of money using extraordinary measures to prolong life for a few weeks when disease is irreversible and death is inevitable and near.

Taking this important step will not solve the huge problems in health care. But it probably would reduce somewhat the amount of money spent on useless, extraordinary measures in the last few weeks and months of life.

In addition to more general things already discussed, there are many additional, more specific, things that can be done to slow down the unacceptable escalation of health care spending.

Medicare and Medicaid currently pay for numerous procedures that have no proven benefit. In 2010 the Food and Drug Administration studied the research and announced that the drug Avastin (which has serious side effects) is not effective in treating breast cancer. But Medicare decided to continue paying for it even though it costs $88,000 a year for each patient.[151] That kind of waste should end.

The two bipartisan commissions, Simpson-Bowles and Domenici-Rivlin, that proposed ways to reduce the deficit both offered significant proposals for reducing health care costs.[152] Medicare has significant co-pays, but most people purchase private "Medigap" policies that pay all or almost all their cost-sharing for Medicare. As a result, people often use health care services when they are not necessary. We should be careful not to add co-pays that discourage poor people from receiving necessary health care, but somewhat larger co-pays for most of us would discourage unnecessary use of doctors, tests and hospitals.[153] That is why both Simpson-Bowles and President Obama have said we should forbid or discourage Medigap policies from providing first dollar wraparound coverage. Medicare recipients themselves should have to pay some initial co-pays to discourage unnecessary use of medical services

Currently, drug companies provide substantial rebates for medicine for people on Medicaid. Medicare should receive the same rebates, at least for low-income people it serves.[154] The full details of the concrete recommendations of the two commissions are too complex to describe briefly. But they all merit careful consideration. If we adopted most of them, they would significantly slow the growth of federal health care costs.

It will be very difficult. But we must set a target of trying to slow the growth of health care costs generally and federal health care costs specifically so that within a reasonable period of time (hopefully no more than ten years) they grow each year no more than growth in GDP plus 0.5% to 1% per beneficiary. We will need some flexibility in the target because epidemics, medical breakthroughs and the results of various demonstration projects bear on how much we can slow cost growth without denying access to health care for the poor and elderly. But we should set a target and do our best to reach it. To do otherwise would be economically foolish.

Especially with regard to Medicare, it is intergenerationally

SAVING MEDICARE AND SLOWING GROWTH
IN HEALTH CARE COSTS

- Move away from fee for service to preventive care
- Provide programs to reduce obesity
- Encourage "living wills" to reduce extraordinary measures when death is inevitable and near
- Limit size of malpractice awards for non-economic and punitive damages
- Modestly increase co-pays for most people to discourage unnecessary use
- Follow the best medical science and stop paying for procedures/medicines that are not effective
- Set a target for a date by which growth in medical costs is no more than growth in GDP plus 0.5% to 1% per beneficiary

Table 5.4.

unjust for today's seniors to demand that our working children and grandchildren spend so much on our health care that they cannot afford to fund quality education, wise research and good infrastructure that will produce a flourishing economy in the future. That is simply unfair. Seniors should take the lead in saying that—loudly, clearly and persistently.

DEFENSE BUDGET

According to the bipartisan taskforce led by Domenici-Rivlin, the U.S. defense budget is roughly as much as the defense budgets of all other countries combined.[155] Domenici-Rivlin proposed that we freeze defense spending for five years and then not let it grow any more than growth in GDP after that. They estimated that would save $1.1 trillion through 2020.[156]

For starters, we could reduce cost overruns. The conservative Heritage Foundation has reported that the federal government's Government Accountability Office (GAO) has uncovered $295 billion in cost overruns in ninety-five weapons systems.[157] Saving much of that $295 billion would help.

In a 2011 article in the prestigious journal *Foreign Affairs*, two prominent American specialists in foreign affairs and defense outlined a number of specific steps that would "cut the Pentagon's budget while improving its performance."[158] They noted that Admiral Mike Mullen, former chairman of the Joint Chiefs of Staff, has warned that "the single biggest threat to our national security is our debt."[159] They also pointed out that the $700 billion spent on national defense in 2011 was twice as much as in 2001—and more in real dollars than for any year since the end of the Second World War. Defense budgets have expanded even though "the United States has never been more secure militarily."[160]

These two specialists outlined detailed ways to cut the defense budget by $788 billion in the seven years from FY2012 to FY2018. Even with those cuts, the United States would still be spending (after adjustments for inflation) in FY2018 considerably more than the average defense expenditures during the Cold War. They concluded that in spite of these cuts the U.S. military would still "be the only force capable of patrolling the world's oceans, deploying hundreds of thousands of ground forces anywhere on the planet, dominating airspace, and managing intelligence and logistics worldwide."[161]

I think we should cut the defense budget by at least $100 billion a year. Perhaps we could learn from Great Britain's Conservative Prime Minister David Cameron. He decided to postpone a costly nuclear submarine program in order to increase the funds for economic foreign aid for poor countries.

As this chapter makes clear, it will not be easy to solve our deficit crisis. But it can be done. And it can be done without slashing effective programs that empower poor neighbors here and around the world.

In summary:

1. We need a balance of reduced expenditures and increased taxes. Chuck Colson is right that there is no biblical warrant

for refusing all tax increases or refusing all program cuts. A balanced 50-50 approach is what I think we need.

2. We can and should cut unnecessary subsidies and useless duplicative programs. We should rigorously evaluate all programs and end or change those that do not work. We can cut the defense budget some without threatening national security. We can make changes in Medicare and social security that produce genuine savings without destroying them through privatization.

3. We also need to increase tax revenues somewhat, apply the payroll tax and the regular income tax rates to investment income, increase the top marginal income tax rate and retain the estate tax.

To those who adamantly oppose all tax increases, my friend Howard Ahmanson offers an interesting response. Howard is a wealthy man, a strong political conservative, a lifelong Republican. He has donated millions of dollars to conservative political causes. But recently he became so disgusted with the refusal of California Republicans to consider any tax increases as the state faced colossal deficits that he took dramatic action that astonished everyone. He registered as a Democrat! Why? Because, as he said in an article in the local paper, the Republican party had narrowed itself down to one article of faith: "no tax shall ever be raised ever ever."[162] Howard's action stunned everyone, producing a spate of news stories. (Howard also asked for my help to contact Democrats for Life so that he could support Democrats who are pro-life.)

Howard would certainly disagree with many of my proposals here. But his attitude reflects what we desperately need. We must have reasonable people from both sides of the political aisle who are willing to analyze our current situation carefully without some dogmatic presupposition of either "no tax cuts" or "no cuts in programs." If we can carefully, honestly evaluate our present dilemma, put all options on the table and then work toward reasonable compromise that is just to the poor and our grandchildren, we can fix our moral deficit.

6

WE CAN DO IT

A wise path forward is fairly clear. There is a way to go that is economically wise and morally just. With a judicious combination of budget cuts and tax increases, we can reduce and then eliminate most budget deficits in a way that will help the economy and be fair to our grandchildren. And we can do that without increasing poverty or slashing effective programs that provide poor neighbors with a helping hand that empowers them to earn a decent living and enjoy quality health care.

The basic framework of a wise, balanced solution is clear. The hard part is creating the political will to do it. Partisan politics today is so divisive that it will be very difficult to find the necessary bipartisan compromises and agreements that will move us forward.

Even as I write this book, both Democrats and Republicans continue to take inconsistent, irresponsible positions that make progress difficult. Almost everyone agrees that we should end many of the tax breaks in the tax code that offer special advantages to particular businesses. There are tax breaks for NASCAR racetrack operators, makers of toy wooden arrows, Eskimo whaling captains and the makers of fishing tackle boxes. These kinds of tax loopholes for large and small businesses cost the government an estimated $123 billion a year. Republican Senator Tom Coburn has rightly denounced them as "little more than corporate welfare."[1] These tax breaks both distort the efficient functioning of the economy and reduce federal tax revenue, thus increasing the deficit. Democrats and Republicans alike say we should abolish these loopholes.

Everyone agrees—except when loopholes are ones the particular politician supports to help special interests in his or her home state. The Senate Republican leader Mitch McConnell calls for ending special tax breaks for special interests—except for the tax breaks for the owners of thoroughbred racehorses in his home state of Kentucky! McConnell helped secure that loophole in 2008 and now says Kentucky needs it to protect jobs.

Democratic Senator John Kerry also loudly calls for ending such loopholes—except when it comes to special tax breaks for small breweries. Kerry is one of the primary supporters of an effort to cut taxes for small beer makers like Adams Brewery in Boston.

Republican Representative Paul Ryan also calls for an end to this kind of loophole. He even has publically distanced himself from a proposed tax break for brewers. Privately, however, he has assured a beer industry group that he would support their proposal.

Or take another example. In 2011, President Obama proposed a tax increase on tax filers making more than $250,000 a year in order to help pay for a program to create jobs and reduce the deficit. But Democratic Senators like Charles E. Schumer insisted that people making $250,000 a year were not actually rich! So he helped persuade the Democratic leaders of the Senate to only propose a tax increase on those making a million dollars or more a year.

This kind of duplicity and foolishness on the part of our political leaders makes our task difficult. But it is not impossible.

It is important to remember that courageous, persistent movements have dramatically changed history.

It took decades of hard, continuous struggle, but William Wilberforce and the movement he created eventually ended the slave trade and then slavery itself throughout the British Empire. Martin Luther King Jr. did not easily or quickly win the battle against segregation. But Dr. King and the large Civil Rights movement he led profoundly changed American history. For decades it seemed that the ghastly evil of apartheid in South Africa was unshakeable. But the persistent campaign of courageous South African leaders like Archbishop Desmond Tutu and Nelson Mandela eventually prevailed—in part because of the support of millions in South Africa and around the world. For decades Marxist governments in Eastern Europe and the Soviet Union seemed invincible. But Solidarity, the daring trade union in Poland, organized an ongoing movement that successfully defied the Soviet Union—and contributed to its collapse. Today, thanks to the bold ongoing efforts of democratic movements in many countries, democracy now flourishes in vastly more nations than just fifty or even thirty years ago. In 2011 courageous protestors in many Arab nations astonished the world and produced historic changes in several countries.

Citizens can correct injustice. We can change unjust policies. It is not easy. It cannot be done in a year or two. To succeed it takes years of commitment by large numbers of people to a just, wise vision. But history proves it can be done.

I dream that Christians and other people of goodwill will resolve to create a movement and work together over the next decade to end our deficit crisis in a way that is economically wise and morally just. Thanks to the precious gift of democratic freedom, we have space to do that. It is true that small numbers of very wealthy people virtually own the politicians in both parties. But if enough of us citizens organize an ongoing movement, we can change the direction of American history.

In fact, it is already beginning to happen. In April 2011 a very broad coalition of Christian leaders joined together to form a "Circle of Protection" around effective programs in the federal budget that assist and empower needy persons both here and abroad.

It started with a Lenten fast led by David Beckman, president of Bread for the World, Jim Wallis, president of Sojourners, and former Congressman Tony Hall. I responded, as did thousands of other Christians around the country, to their invitation to join the fast and sign the call to Congress to protect vital programs for poor people here and around the world. Their statement to President Obama and the Congress agreed that we must deal with the federal deficit. But "budgets are moral documents, and how we reduce future deficits are historic and defining moral choices." A crucial moral measure of every budget is how it treats the most poor and vulnerable. "We look at every budget proposal from the bottom up—how it treats those Jesus called 'the least of these' (Matthew 25:45)." Therefore, the statement said, "we urge Congress and the administration to give moral priority to programs that protect the life and dignity of poor and vulnerable people in these difficult times."

Top leaders in the National Association of Evangelicals, the U.S. Conference of Catholic Bishops, the Salvation Army, Sojourners, the National Hispanic Christian Leadership Conference, Evangelicals for Social Action and the National Council of Churches have joined the Circle of Protection. More than thirteen thousand Americans added their signatures within a short time. Scores of media outlets (including the *New York Times* and *Time* magazine) have run stories. And the leaders of the Circle of Protection have pressed their concerns in face-to-face meetings with the President and top Democratic and Republican members of Congress.

The Circle of Protection has already made a difference. When the FY2011 budget was finally passed in mid 2011, the cuts to effective programs for poor people were not as deep as proposed. And when the President and the Congress agreed on a formula to raise the debt ceiling, they appointed a "super committee" of twelve senators and congresspersons who were given the task of agreeing on ways to substantially reduce the deficit. If they failed, the agreement said (and they did!), then both the defense budget and other discretionary programs would face automatic dramatic budget cuts. But they also agreed that a number of key programs assisting poor people would not be subject to these automatic cuts. It is generally thought that that crucial arrangement protecting the poor was due in a major way to the Circle of Protection.

We must strengthen and expand the Circle of Protection for the ongoing historic debate. Bread for the World president David Beckman underlines how serious our historic choice is: "Everything we have achieved for poor and hungry people in the last 35 years is under severe threat of budget cuts."[2] To join the Circle of Protection and add your signature, go to www .evangelicalsforsocialaction.org.

In the spring of 2011, Evangelicals for Social Action (in cooperation with the Center for Public Justice) launched "A Call for Intergenerational Justice: A Christian Proposal on the American Debt Crisis." We acknowledged that our "current culture of debt threatens to bankrupt us both economically and morally." Ongoing, ever-continuing federal deficits are unacceptable. But how we make the necessary changes is crucial. "To reduce our federal debt at the expense of our poorest fellow citizens would be a violation of the biblical teaching that God has a special concern for the poor."

The call especially emphasizes the issue of intergenerational justice. We are presently putting current expenditures on our grandchildren's credit cards. To continue doing that is unfair.

To the young, we say: It is your credit card that will receive the additional trillions of dollars of debt—unless we quickly end ongoing federal budget deficits. To parents and grandparents, we say: We must give up some things so our children can flourish. All of us now say: We join together to answer the call to intergenerational justice.

I invite you to join this movement for justice for the poor now and justice for the next generation. You can add your name to the many who have already signed the Call for Intergenerational Justice (go to www.evangelicalsforsocialaction.org). You can form a study-action group in your church, college or place of work. We hope that many study-action groups will include both seniors and youth.

Together, we can form a growing, powerful movement that if sustained over a decade will avoid economic disaster and promote justice. To do that, we must remember how much is at stake: both the ability to live and thrive now for many hundreds of millions of needy people here and abroad, and the possibility of a decent future for our grandchildren.

The story of Pauline and her children underlines the importance of the historic debate raging in our country. Pauline is a personal friend and active participant in my local church. Her story provides a vivid, concrete example of a poor family that has struggled hard against great odds and is making it—thanks to their own determination, a supportive church and many helpful government programs.

After Pauline graduated from Junior College in 1977, she worked for the next six years. Then she lost her job and could not find work, so she had to go on welfare. In 1990 she moved into "The Village," a public housing project with very low (government subsidized) rent. Even though she had three very young children to care for as a single mother, she tried to go back to school to take a refresher course so she could find another job as a secretary. She wanted her children to see that their mother was working. But it proved impossible to get three children to daycare, then go to classes and then return home to collect the children. So she stayed at home for a number of years, trying to be a good mom and surviving on her welfare checks, food stamps and health insurance via Medicaid.

Life was tough. But Pauline instilled a passion for education in each of her children. She knew that was the only way they could escape a life of poverty.

In 2000, Pauline discovered she had cancer. Fortunately, Medicaid enabled her to receive good medical care. But the cancer and the daily trips for radiation therapy and weekly trips for chemotherapy overwhelmed her. She was too exhausted to take care of some important things. She fell behind on her rent and was threatened with eviction unless she quickly paid $1,700. Desperate, she went downtown to explore emergency help from two government programs. On the way to the second office, she told me, she was so exhausted from the cancer that she begged God to giver her the strength just to keep putting one foot ahead of the other so she could make it to the office. Fortunately, she received the help she needed and her family was not thrown out on the street.

Pauline's cancer left her so weakened that she could not work. She tried several jobs but was so exhausted that she could not continue. Fortunately, food stamps and disability payments through social security enabled her to survive, and Medicaid provided health coverage for her and her children.

Slowly, Pauline started to work as a volunteer in my church's holistic community center—just a few hours a week at first in the after-school program, and then as her strength returned, more hours in the summer camp. She realized she was getting stronger, so she took a job in 2010 working in the census. Then after a short time, she felt ready to take a job working more than half-time in a daycare center. The effects of the cancer are still there, but Pauline is proud that she is now earning more of her own money. Her disability payments have been cut a lot, but she still receives some income there and Medicaid provides ongoing health care.

Pauline even managed to move out of the public housing project in 2011. She proudly told me about the house she rents with the help of the government's section 8 housing program. She has a basement and her own yard—something never available in the Village. With proud joy she told me, "I live just like my neighbors." The day before I talked to her about her journey, Pauline learned of a government program that provides subsidies to lower-income people like herself to purchase a house. She now dreams of owning her own home.

All of Pauline's three children are doing well. They all have embraced their mother's persistent teaching that education is the way out of poverty. All three are high school grads. Her oldest finished junior college and now works for a large transportation company. Her youngest works full time and is about to complete trade school with a certificate as a medical assistant.

I know her middle child, Courtney, best. She has a wonderful gift of liturgical dance, which she uses to bless our church. She has also volunteered at our community center, where I serve on the board.

Courtney remembers her family's tough struggles when she was young. With tears in her eyes she told me how her mother sometimes ate very little so her children could have enough food. Courtney remembers the embarrassment of buying food with the very visible food stamps and the discomfort of old clothes when her classmates in school had name brand clothes and running shoes. Already, by the age of six, Courtney was determined to do well in school so she could work her way out of poverty.

After high school Courtney went to Eastern Mennonite University in Virginia. That would have been totally impossible financially except that she received Pell Grants every year, plus government subsidized Stafford loans, plus income from the federal Work Study program for college students. Even so, she had to drop out for one semester to earn money so she could complete her bachelor's degree—a first for her family.

For one year (2011-2012), Courtney is working full time as a hall director at Virginia Union University, earning money to pay off college loans. But she plans to take her GREs next year and go to graduate school. Her dream is to do a master's degree (and perhaps a Ph.D.) in education. Then she wants to return to an urban setting to work in public education to help other young people realize the same success she has achieved. "I promised myself," she told me, "that I would work hard to help others get a good education so they could work their way out of poverty the way I did."

My friends Pauline and Courtney plead with us not to cut the Pell Grants, food stamps, disability payments, housing support, subsidized college loans and other effective government programs that have enabled them to work their way up out of grinding poverty. I hope and pray that we listen.

ACTION STEPS

To help solve our moral deficit, you can do some things easily and quickly. Others are more complicated and take more time. Start with some easy steps and then tackle more challenging tasks.

1. Read and reflect on a few dozen of the hundreds of biblical verses about God and the poor. Then prayerfully ask God to help you share God's love for poor, hurting persons. If you need help finding the verses, see the two hundred pages of biblical texts on the poor in Ronald J. Sider, *For They Shall Be Fed: Scripture Readings and Prayers for a Just World* (Nashville: Word, 1997) or just go through the dozens of verses in chapter three of Ronald J. Sider, *Rich Christians in an Age of Hunger* (Nashville: Thomas Nelson, 2005).

2. Go to www.evangelicalsforsocialaction.org, join ESA's campaign "Fixing the Moral Deficit" and sign "A Call for Intergenerational Justice: A Christian Proposal on the American Debt Crisis." You can join thousands of others demanding that Washington end our ongoing budget deficits in a way that helps, not hurts, poor people.

3. Join the Circle of Protection (www.circleofprotection.us)

and pledge to resist budget cuts that threaten the essential needs of hungry and poor people at home and abroad.

4. Organize a "Come and See" event by inviting your legislator to visit a service agency in your community that is placed at risk by budget cuts. Invite this person to meet the people affected by these cuts (http://go.sojo.net/comeandsee).

5. Make a small (or large!) regular donation to some program working with and empowering people in poverty, or advocating for greater economic justice.

6. Volunteer your time and talents with an organization working to overcome poverty and injustice.

7. Invite a small circle of friends in your church, college or neighborhood to read this book with you, discussing it and asking what you might do together to implement its concerns. Consider making the study group intergenerational— ask a few seniors, a few youth and a few middle-age people to join the group.

8. Ask your pastor if you or someone else could lead a church study group or Sunday school class on this book and topic. Then discuss how your denomination could better understand and work on this issue.

9. Become a partner in an organization that works nationally to promote justice for poor people here and abroad. Bread for the World (www.bread.org) is a Christian organization with a long, outstanding track record of persuading Washington to improve and adequately fund good programs to empower poor people both here and around the world. Evangelicals for Social Action (www.evangelicalsforsocialaction.org), which I serve as president, has been working almost forty years to promote biblical justice here and abroad.

10. Call or write a letter to your Senators, your congressperson in the House of Representatives and the President urging them to resolve the deficit crisis in a balanced, just way. To find out the names and ways to contact your elected officials, go to www.evangelicalsforsocialaction.org, www.con tactingthecongress.org or www.congressmerge.com.

11. Organize a group to meet with your political representatives, when they are home for recess, to talk with them about what you would like them to do to solve the deficit crisis. To contact them, see suggestion 10.

12. Vote regularly (register to vote if you are not registered). Then think and pray about how to make the issues of this book one of your important concerns as you decide how to vote in local, state and national elections.

13. Consider coming to Palmer Theological Seminary at Eastern University (www.palmerseminary.edu), where I teach, and taking the master's in theological studies with a concentration on Christian faith and public policy.

14. Consider running for office so you can advocate in the halls of political power for a biblically balanced agenda, including the issues discussed in this book.

15. Write letters to your local paper, write a blog, contribute to online forums, start a Facebook page or find other ways to share your views and dialogue (respectfully!) on how to balance the budget in a fair way.

16. Help to change our nation's "culture of debt." Explore ways to simplify your own lifestyle and reduce personal debt.

17. Become better educated on sound financial management and help educate others. Support a class on economic literacy at your church or a local nonprofit.

18. Keep yourself informed (via newspaper, TV, advocacy groups) about upcoming budget decisions in Washington and your state legislature. Be alert to potential decisions that would hurt poor people, and urge your political representatives to oppose them.

NOTES

Chapter 1: The Crisis Is Real

[1]Domenici-Rivlin, p. 12.

[2]The key issue is whether the federal government continuously borrows so much that the national debt *increases* as a percent of GDP. Most economists think that if the government runs a smaller deficit so that, as the economy grows, the total national debt *decreases* as a percent of GDP, there is no economic problem. Nonetheless, I would prefer that the federal government move, over a reasonably short time, to a pattern where we normally (except in times of recession) do not have a budget deficit.

[3]Mindy R. Levit, "The Federal Budget: Issues for FY2011, FY2012, and Beyond," CRS R41685, October 13, 2011, p. 18.

[4]See the July 20, 2011, letter to President Obama and other political leaders from prominent economists who won the Nobel Price; Michelle Bazie, "Nobel Laureates and Leading Economists Oppose Constitutional Balanced Budget Amendment," CBPP, July 28, 2011.

[5]"Monthly Statement of the Public Debt of the United States, Table I—Summary of Treasury Securities Outstanding, October 31, 2011," Bureau of the Public Debt, www.treasurydirect.gov/govt/reports/pd/mspd/2011/opds102011.pdf.

[6]"Monthly Statement of the Public Debt, Historical Information," Bureau of the Public Debt, www.treasurydirect.gov/govt/reports/pd/mspd/mspd.htm.

[7]"CBO's 2011 Long Term Budget Outlook," CBO, June 2011, p. 1.

[8]Mindy R. Levit, "The Federal Debt: An Analysis of Movements from World War II to the Present," CRS RL34712, September 17, 2010, p. 19.

[9]"Foreign Holdings of Federal Debt," CRS R522331, March 25, 2011, p. 2.

[10]Kathy A. Ruffing and James R. Horney, "Economic Downturn and Bush Policies Continue to Drive Large Projected Deficits," CBPP, May 10, 2011, p. 1.

[11]Levit, "Federal Budget," CRS R41685.

[12]Mindy R. Levit, "Mandatory Spending Since 1962," CRS RL33074, February 16, 2010, p. 4.

[13]There is, of course, a huge difference between expenditures that seniors want for themselves now (e.g., social security, Medicare) and expenditures (e.g., for education, research and infrastructure) that will actually increase the economic well-being of their children and grandchildren.

[14]Marc Labonte, "The Economic Implications of the Long-Term Federal Budget Outlook," CRS RL32747, August 27, 2008, p. 13.

[15]Sarah E. Zylstra, "Shrinking Circle of Protection," *Christianity Today*, August 2011, p. 15.

Chapter 2: Crucial Economic Data: "Just the Facts, Ma'am"
[1]"Today's Census Report in Pictures," *Off the Charts*, CBPP, September 13, 2011, www.offthechartsblog.org/today%E2%80%99s-census-report-in-pictures.

[2]See note 5 of this chapter.

[3]For a detailed response to this argument see Ronald J. Sider, *Just Generosity*, 2nd ed. (Grand Rapids: Baker, 2009), pp. 37-40.

[4]Indivar Dutta-Gupta, "Why the Upcoming Poverty Numbers Matter," *Off the Charts*, CBPP, September 12, 2011, www.offthechartsblog.org/why-the-upcoming-poverty-numbers-matter.

[5]See the summary of the Census Bureau report in the *New York Times*, September 14, 2011, pp. A1, A19, and the CBPP's "Poverty Rate Second-Highest in 45 Years; Record Numbers Lacked Health Insurance, Lived in Deep Poverty," September 14, 2011.

[6]Tami Luhby, "Poverty Rate Rises Under Alternative Census Measure," *CNN Money*, November 7, 2011, http://money.cnn.com/2011/11/07/news/economy/poverty_rate/index.htm.

[7]G. William Domhoff, "Wealth, Income and Power," UC Santa Cruz, September 2005, www2.ucsc.edu/whorulesamerica/power/wealth.html.

[8]Hannah Shaw and Chad Stone, "Tax Data Show Richest 1 Percent Took a Hit in 2008, but Income Remained Highly Concentrated at the Top," CBPP, October 21, 2010, p. 3.

[9]"Poverty in 2010 Hit 52-Year High, U.S. Says," *New York Times*, September 14, 2011, p. A19.

[10]Avi Feller and Chuck Marr, "Tax Rate for Richest 400 Taxpayers Plummeted in Recent Decades, Even as Their Pre-Tax Incomes Skyrocketed," CBPP, February 23, 2010, pp. 1-2.

[11]CBO data in Arloc Shermon and Chad Stone, "Income Gaps Between Very Rich and Everyone Else More Than Tripled in Last Three Decades, New Data Show," CBPP, June 25, 2010, p. 4.

[12]Don Peck, "Can the Middle Class Be Saved?" *Atlantic*, September 2011, www.theatlantic.com/magazine/archive/2011/09/can-the-middle-class-be-saved/8600. See also Avi Feller and Chad Stone, "Top 1 Percent of Americans Reaped Two-Thirds of Income Gains in Last Economic Expansion," CBPP, September 9, 2009, www.cbpp.org/files/9-9-09pov.pdf (based on Piketty-Saez).

[13]Shaw and Stone, "Tax Data," p. 2.

[14]Ibid.

[15]Brian W. Cashell, "Inequality in the Distribution of Income," CRS RL32639, October 19, 2009, p. 8.

[16]Domhoff, "Wealth, Income and Power."

[17]Rakesh Kochhar, Richard Fry and Paul Taylor, "Wealth Gaps Rise to Record Highs Between Whites, Blacks, Hispanics," Pew Research Center, July 26, 2011, www.pewsocialtrends.org/2011/07/26/wealth-gaps-rise-to -record-highs-between-whites-blacks-hispanics/#executive-summary.

[18]Edward N. Wolff, "Recent Trends in Household Wealth in the United States: Rising Debt and the Middle-class Squeeze," Levy Economics Institute of Bard College, June 2007, p. 15.

[19]Domhoff, "Wealth, Income and Power."

[20]Rana Foroohar, "What Ever Happened to Upward Mobility?" *Time*, November 14, 2011, pp. 26-31.

[21]"More Compensation Heading to the Very Top," Economic Policy Institute, www.stateofworkingamerica.org/charts/view/17.

[22]Sarah Anderson et al., "Executive Excess 2011: The Massive CEO Rewards for Tax Dodging," Institute for Policy Studies, August 31, 2011, www.ips-dc. org/reports/executive_excess_2011_the_massive_ceo_rewards_for_tax_ dodging. At times the ratio has been even higher. In 2005 the ratio of CEO pay at Fortune 500 companies to average production workers was 411:1, and at the height of the stock market bubble in 2000, it was 531:1 (compared to 42:1 in 1980)! (See Sarah Anderson et al., "Executive Excess 2006," ed. Sam Pizzigati, Institute for Policy Studies and United for a Fair Economy, August 30, 2006, www.ips-dc.org/files/155/ExecutiveExcess2006.pdf.

[23]Nelson D. Schwartz and Louise Story, "Pay of Hedge Fund Managers Roared Back Last Year," *New York Times*, March 31, 2010, www.nytimes. com/2010/04/01/business/01hedge.html.

[24]L. McCall and C. Percheski, "Income Inequality: New Trends and Research Directions," *Annual Review of Sociology* 36 (2010): 329-47.

[25]Alice Gomstyn, "Walmart CEO Pay: More in an Hour Than Workers Get All Year?" *ABC News*, July 2, 2010, http://abcnews.go.com/Business/walmart -ceo-pay-hour-workers-year/story?id=11067470. Michael Duke, CEO of

Walmart, had a salary of $28 million in 2008, which works out to $13,462 per hour. Employees who earn $8.75 an hour make $13,650 a year.

[26]Sanjai Bhagat and Brian Bolton, "Bank Executive Compensation and Capital Requirements Reform," University of Colorado at Boulder and University of New Hampshire, January 2011, http://leeds-faculty.colorado.edu/bhagat/BankComp-Capital-Jan2011.pdf.

[27]Sarah Anderson et al, "CEO Pay and the Great Recession: 17th Annual Executive Compensation Survey," Institute for Policy Studies, September 1, 2010, www.ips-dc.org/files/2433/EE-2010-web.pdf.

[28]Ibid.

[29]"Wealth Inequality," Inequality.org, http://inequality.org/wealth-inequality. The top 1% earn 20%, the bottom 50% only about 13%. See also Paul Van de Water et al., "'Supercommittee' Should Develop Balanced Package of Tax Increases and Spending Cuts," CBPP, September 27, 2011, p. 2, www.cbpp.org/files/9-27-11tax.pdf.

[30]Peter Whoriskey, "With Executive Pay, Rich Pull Away from Rest of America," Washington Post, June 18, 2011.

[31]Nicole Neroulias, Religion News Service, April 4, 2011.

[32]Dan Ariely, "Wealth Inequality," Danariely.com, September 30, 2010, http://danariely.com/2010/09/30/wealth-inequality.

[33]Chuck Collins, "We're Not Broke, Just Twisted," Inequality.org, May 12, 2011, http://inequality.org/notbroke.

[34]David L. Brumbaugh and Don. C Richards, "The Level of Taxes in the United States, 1940-2003," CRS RS20087, July 6, 2004, p. 4.

[35]Ethan Pollack and Rebecca Thiess, "Taxes on the Wealthy Have Gone Down Dramatically," Economic Policy Institute, April 14, 2011, www.epi.org/publication/taxes_on_the_wealthy_have_gone_down_dramatically.

[36]Feller and Marr, "Tax Rate," p. 1.

[37]Robert J. Samuelson, "The Real Tax Avoidance Scandal," Washington Post, April 3, 2011.

[38]Feller and Marr, "Tax Rate."

[39]CBO data cited in Sherman and Stone, "Income Gaps."

[40]Thomas L. Hungerford, "Income Inequality and the U.S. Tax System," CRS RL34155, September 4, 2007, p. 9.

[41]Chuck Marr, "Yes, There's Real Money at the Top," Off the Charts, CBPP, August 18, 2011, www.offthechartsblog.org/yes-there's-real-money-at-the-top.

[42]Ibid.

[43]Carola Frydman and Raven E. Saks, "Historical Trends in Executive Compensation 1936-2003," November 15, 2005, http://faculty.chicagobooth.edu/workshops/AppliedEcon/archive/pdf/FrydmanSecondPaper.pdf.

[44]Robert Reich, *Aftershock: The Next Economy and America's Future* (New York: Vintage, 2010), p. 132; Reich uses the years 1983 to 2007 for the second period.

[45]Ibid., p. 45.

[46]Rana Foroohar, "Struck in the Middle," *Time*, August 15, 2011, p. 26; and Michael Kumhof and Romain Rancière, "Leveraging Inequality," *Finance & Development* 47, no. 4 (2010): 28-31.

[47]Andrew G. Berg and Jonathan D. Ostry, "Equality and Efficiency," *Finance & Development* 48, no. 3 (2011), www.imf.org/external/pubs/ft/fandd/2011/09/Berg.htm.

[48]See Cashell, "Inequality, pp. 10ff.

[49]See also Paul Krugman, "The Social Contract," *New York Times*, September 22, 2011.

Chapter 3: The Big Questions in the Debate

[1]See Rand's collection of essays *The Virtue of Selfishness: A New Concept of Egoism* (New York: Penguin, 1964). The quote is from a 1979 television interview with Phil Donahue.

[2]Onkar Ghate, "Does America Need Ayn Rand or Jesus?," Foxnews.com, June 29, 2011, www.foxnews.com/opinion/2011/06/29/does-america-need-ayn-rand-or-jesus.

[3]Chuck Colson, "The Legacy of Ayn Rand," *Townhall.com*, October 16, 2007.

[4]Vincent Miller, "Ayn Rand, Paul Ryan and an Ideology Never Challenged," in *All Things*, April 22, 2011. Marvin Olasky says Paul Ryan recommends Rand's *Atlas Shrugged* "apparently without caveat" ("Take a Stand Against Rand," *World*, July 16, 2011).

[5]Michael Gerson, "Ayn Rand's Adult-Onset Adolescence," *Washington Post*, April 21, 2011.

[6]Jose Miranda, *Marx and the Bible* (Maryknoll, N.Y.: Orbis, 1974), p. 48.

[7]Ronald J. Sider, *For They Shall Be Fed* (Dallas: Word, 1997), which has two hundred pages of biblical texts, and chapter three of Ronald J. Sider, *Rich Christians in an Age of Hunger* (Nashville: Nelson, 2005).

[8]On God acting on behalf of the poor, see the texts in *Rich Christians*, pp. 42-48. On God response to oppressors and the stingy, see *Rich Christians*, pp. 52-56.

[9]See the examples noted in Ronald J. Sider, *The Scandal of Evangelical Politics* (Grand Rapids: Baker, 2008), p. 263 nn. 13-14.

[10]E. Calvin Beisner, *Prosperity and Poverty* (Westchester, Ill.: Crossway, 1988), p. 54.

[11]For a longer discussion, see Sider, *Scandal of Evangelical Politics*, pp. 106-17.

[12]See the numerous texts cited in ibid., pp. 123-24.

[13]In Marxist societies, where private ownership is abolished, political and economic power are combined in a way that almost guarantees totalitarianism.

[14]Mohamed El-Erian, quoted in Nicholas D. Kristof, "Crony Capitalism Comes Home," *New York Times*, October 27, 2011, p. A25.

[15]Tim King, "Family Research Council Attacks Evangelical and Catholic Leaders," *God's Politics* (blog), July 29, 2011, http://blog.sojo.net/2011/07/29/family-research-council-attacks-evangelical-and-catholic-leaders.

[16]Ayn Rand, "The Question of Scholarships," *The Objectivist*, June 1966, p. 11. See a response to this view from a conservative perspective in Gerson, "Ayn Rand's Adult-Onset Adolescence."

[17]Scott McConnell, *100 Voices: An Oral History of Ayn Rand* (New York: NAL Trade, 2010); Joshua Holland, "Ayn Rand Railed Against Government Benefits, But Grabbed Social Security and Medicare When She Needed Them," *AlterNet*, January 29, 2011, www.alternet.org/teaparty/149721/ayn_rand_railed_against_government_benifits%2C_but_grabbed_social_security_and_medicare_when_she_needed_them.

[18]The following paragraph is from Sider, *Scandal of Evangelical Politics*, p. 124.

[19]John Mason, "Assisting the Poor: Assistance Programmes in the Bible," *Transformation*, April-June 1987, p. 9 (see all of pp. 1-14).

[20]Ronald J. Sider and Diane Knippers, *Toward an Evangelical Public Policy* (Grand Rapids: Baker, 2005), p. 366.

[21]See chap. 5, p. 89.

[22]Estimates for 2010 by D. Andrew Austin and Mindy R. Levit, "Mandatory Spending," CRS RL33074, February 16, 2010, p. 6.

[23]Wayne Grudem, *Politics According to the Bible* (Grand Rapids: Zondervan, 2010), p. 281.

Chapter 4: Current Proposals: Simply Not Good Enough

[1]Tobin Grant, "NAE: Reduce Debt, but Protect Poor," *Christianity Today*, March 21, 2011, http://blog.christianitytoday.com/ctpolitics/2011/03/nae_reduce_debt.html.

[2]"Testimony of Robert Greenstein," CBPP, July 26, 2011, pp. 3, 10.

[3]Stuart Butler, "Should the Disadvantaged Be Spared from the Budget Axe?" *Heritage Foundation*, March 8, 2011, www.heritage.org/research/reports/2011/03/should-the-disadvantaged-be-spared-from-the-budget-axe.

[4]Simpson-Bowles, p. 25.

[5]See chap. 5 n. 157.

[6]Senator Tom Coburn, *Wastebook 2010*, December 2010, http://coburn
.senate.gov/public//index.cfm?a=Files.Serve&File_id=4a184ddb-cd85
-4052-b38b-5a1116acca8c.

[7]Nicole Neroulias, "Survey," Religion News Service, April 20, 2011.

[8]Simpson-Bowles, p. 28.

[9]Domenici-Rivlin, p. 94.

[10]Ibid.; Simpson-Bowles, p. 21.

[11]Simpson-Bowles, p. 11.

[12]Thomas Donohue, "The Highway to Jobs—Via Better Infrastructure,"
Christian Science Monitor, September 8, 2011, www.csmonitor.com/com
mentary/opinion/2011/0908/The-highway-to-jobs-via-better-infrastructure.

[13]This is the recommendation of Domenici-Rivlin, p. 21.

[14]"The Budget Deals of Reagan, Bush, Clinton and Obama, in One Chart,"
Washington Post, July 7, 2011, www.washingtonpost.com/blogs/ezra-klein
/post/the-budget-deals-of-reagan-bush-clinton-and-obama-in-one-chart
/2011/07/06/gIQA98w11H_blog.html.

[15]"Testimony of Robert Greenstein," CBPP, July 26, 2011.

[16]Simpson-Bowles, p. 12.

[17]Mindy R. Levit, "Reducing the Budget Deficit," CRS R41784, April 19, 2011.

[18]David Brooks, "Moment of Truth," *Washington Post*, April 4, 2011, www
.nytimes.com/2011/04/05/opinion/05brooks.html?hp.

[19]This category of spending excludes mandatory entitlement programs like
social security, Medicare/Medicaid and food stamps, as well as defense
spending.

[20]"Appendix: Overlapping Policies and Estimated Savings Across Fiscal
Plans," in *What We Hope to See from the Super Committee*, CRFB, September
7, 2011; Robert Greenstein, "Chairman Ryan Gets Nearly Two-Thirds of
His Huge Budget Cuts From Programs for Lower-Income Americans,"
CBPP, April 20, 2011, www.cbpp.org/cms/?fa=view&id=3451; Dottie
Rosenbaum, "Ryan Budget Would Slash SNAP Funding by $127 Billion
Over Ten Years," CBPP, April 11, 2011, www.cbpp.org/cms/index.cfm?fa=
view&id=3463.

[21]See chap. 5, p. 94.

[22]"Ryan Medicaid Block Grant," CBPP, May 3, 2011.

[23]Robert Greenstein, "CBO Report: Ryan Plan Specifies Spending Path That
Would Nearly End Most of Government Other Than Social Security, Health
Care, and Defense by 2050," CBPP, April 7, 2011, www.cbpp.org/cms/
index.cfm?fa=view&id=3453.

[24]See the analysis in CBPP, April 20, 2011, and CBPP, April 5, 2011.

[25]James Horney, "Ryan Budget Plan Produces Far Less Real Deficit Cutting Than Reported," CBPP, April 8, 2011, www.cbpp.org/cms/index.cfm?fa=view&id=3458.

[26]"Long-Term Analysis of a Budget Proposal by Chairman Ryan," CBO, April 5, 2011, p. 3, www.cbo.gov/ftpdocs/121xx/doc12128/04-05-Ryan_Letter.pdf. It would, however, largely eliminate the debt by 2050.

[27]CBPP, July 27, 2011.

[28]"Honest Solutions," Republican Study Committee, April 2011.

[29]I include in this discussion both Obama's proposed FY2012 budget and his proposal for deficit reduction on September 19, 2011.

[30]For Obama, see Mindy R. Levit, "The Federal Budget," CRS R41685, March 11, 2011, p. 14; and Mindy R. Levit, "Impact on the Federal Budget," CRS R41174, March 22, 2011, p. 4. For Ryan, see Concurrent Resolution on the Budget—Fiscal Year 2012, Report of the Committee on the Budget, House of Representatives, "The Path to Prosperity: Restoring America's Promise," April 5, 2011, pp. 5-6.

[31]"Factbox," Reuters, April 14, 2011.

[32]For Ryan, see CRFB, "Appendix: Overlapping Policies," p. 7; for Obama, see "Living Within Our Means and Investing in the Future: The President's Plan for Economic Growth and Deficit Reduction," Office of Management and Budget, September 19, 2011, www.whitehouse.gov/sites/default/files/omb/budget/fy2012/assets/jointcommitteereport.pdf.

[33]CRFB, "Appendix: Overlapping Policies," p. 8, and "Living Within Our Means," Office of Management and Budget.

[34]James R. Horney, "Statement: James R. Horney, Vice President of Federal Fiscal Policy, on President Obama's Budget Package," CBPP, September 19, 2011, www.cbpp.org/cms/index.cfm?fa=view&id=3584.

[35]"Living Within Our Means and Investing in the Future," p. 4; "Overall, These Proposals [including the Affordable Care Act] Will Save $248 Billion in Medicare Over 10 Years and $73 Billion in Medicaid and Other Health Programs," OMB, www.whitehouse.gov/sites/default/files/omb/budget/fy2012/assets/jointcommitteereport.pdf.

[36]Robert Pear, "Obama Proposes $320 Billion in Medicare and Medicaid Cuts Over 10 Years," New York Times, September 20, 2011, p. A16.

[37]Levit, "Impact on the Federal Budget," p. 7.

[38]Quoted in Thomas L. Friedman, "Are We Going to Roll Up Our Sleeves or Limp On?" New York Times, September 21, 2011, p. A27.

[39]Office of the Press Secretary, "Fact Sheet," April 13, 2011. In his September 19, 2011, proposals, the mix was 60-40 according to a New York Times editorial dated September 20, 2011, p. A26.

[40]"If You're Not Serious About the Deficit, You Cannot Spare the Middle Class" (editorial), *USA Today*, May 13-15, 2011, p. 7W.

[41]CRFB, "Appendix: Overlapping Policies," p. 2. That is not to say that Ryan's specific proposal is the way to do it. Peter Orszag worked in the Obama administration but now criticizes President Obama for failing to pursue malpractice reform. See Orszag's proposals at "How Health Care Can Save or Sink America," *Foreign Affairs*, www.foreignaffairs.com/articles/67918/peter-r-orszag/how-health-care-can-save-or-sink-america.

[42]Simpson-Bowles, p. 39.

[43]CRFB, "Appendix: Overlapping Policies," p. 8. It is true that Obama's proposal—a ceiling of 28 cents on the dollar for the value of all itemized deductions in general—does not only apply to charitable deductions, but I think the restriction on charitable deductions is a mistake.

Chapter 5: A Better Way

[1]Some think the proper goal is only reducing budget deficits to the point where the federal debt does not grow any faster than the economy. I prefer to move toward a situation where budget deficits are the exception, not the norm, but that does not mean a balanced budget amendment. Sometimes, deficits are necessary and desirable.

[2]See for example Bread for the World's critique of aspects of earlier American foreign aid; "Phasing Out Monetization" in chapter four of their "2012 Hunger Report."

[3]"Policy Basics," CBPP, March 21, 2011.

[4]BFW, "2012 Hunger Report," chap. 2.

[5]Ibid.

[6]Ryan, "Path to Prosperity," p. 41.

[7]Dorothy Rosenbaum, "House-Passed Proposal," CBPP, June 7, 2011, p. 5.

[8]Ibid., p. 1.

[9]"Policy Basics: Introduction to the Supplemental Nutrition Assistance Program (SNAP)," CBPP, March 21, 2011, www.cbpp.org/cms/index.cfm?fa=view&id=2226.

[10]Rosenbaum, "House-Passed Proposal," p. 5.

[11]BFW, "2012 Hunger Report," chap. 2.

[12]"Statement: Robert Greenstein," CBPP, September 13, 2011, p. 4. The official definition of the poverty level does not count noncash income like SNAP and EITC. But the Census Bureau also said that if we use a different definition that includes noncash income, then SNAP lifted 3.9 million people out of poverty in 2010.

[13]Zoë Neuberger, "Will WIC Turn Away Eligible Low-Income Women and

Children Next Year?" CBPP, September 19, 2011.

[14]"Briefing Rooms: The WIC Program," Economic Research Service, March 21, 2011, www.ers.usda.gov/Briefing/WIC.

[15]L. E. Hicks and R. A. Langham, "Cognitive Measure Stability in Siblings Following Early Nutritional Supplementation," *Public Health Report* 100, no. 6 (1985): 656-62, www.ncbi.nlm.nih.gov/pmc/articles/PMC1425315.

[16]BFW, "2012 Hunger Report," chap. 2.

[17]Dorothy Rosenbaum and Zoë Neuberger, "Food and Nutrition Programs: Reducing Hunger, Bolstering Nutrition," CBPP, August 17, 2005, www.cbpp.org/files/7-19-05fa.pdf.

[18]BFW, "2012 Hunger Report," chap. 2.

[19]"Tina's Story about WIC," *Halfinten.org*, June 30, 2011, http://halfinten.org/stories/tinas-story-about-wic.

[20]Neuberger, "Will WIC Turn Away?"

[21]These include Head Start, the Emergency Food Assistance Program, and Commodity Distribution Program.

[22]"National School Lunch Program," USDA, October 2011, www.fns.usda.gov/cnd/lunch/AboutLunch/NSLPFactSheet.pdf.

[23]David Beckman, *Exodus from Hunger* (Louisville: Westminster John Knox, 2010), p. 11.

[24]"About EITC," Internal Revenue Service, January 18, 2010, www.eitc.irs.gov/central/abouteitc.

[25]Nicholas Johnson and Erica Williams, "A Hand Up," CBPP, April 2011, p. 6.

[26]"Anna's Story About the EITC," *Halfinten.org*, April 18, 2011, http://halfinten.org/stories/anna-davis-story-about-the-eitc.

[27]"Policy Basics: The Earned Income Tax Credit," CBPP, September 6, 2011, www.cbpp.org/cms/index.cfm?fa=view&id=2505.

[28]Stephen D. Holt, "The Earned Income Tax Credit at Age 30," Brookings Institute, February 2006, pp. 9-10. See the literature cited there on the success of the EITC.

[29]Ibid.

[30]Nicholas Johnson and Erica Williams, "A Hand Up: How State Earned Income Tax Credits Help Working Families Escape Poverty in 2011," CBPP, April 2011, p. 8.

[31]Editorial, "Don't Gut Pell Grants," *Washington Post*, July 16, 2011, www.washingtonpost.com/opinions/dont-gut-pell-grants/2011/07/05/gIQA2R InII_story.html.

[32]"2009–2010 Federal Pell Grant Program End-of-Year Report," U.S. Department of Education, Office of Postsecondary Education, www2.ed.gov/finaid/prof/resources/data/pell-2009-10/pell-eoy-09-10.pdf.

[33]"Don't Gut Pell Grants."

[34]Eric Bettinger, "How Financial Aid Affects Persistence," National Bureau of Economic Research, September 2004, www.nber.org/chapters/c10101; Sarah Goldrick-Rab et al., "Conditional Cash Transfers and College Persistence: Evidence from a Randomized Need-Based Grant Program," Institute for Research on Poverty, Discussion Paper no. 1393-11, University of Wisconsin-Madison, July 7, 2011, www.finaidstudy.org/documents/Goldrick-Rab%20Harris%20Benson%20Kelchen.pdf; and Sandy Baum, Michael McPherson, and Patricia Steele, eds., *The Effectiveness of Student Aid Policies: What the Research Tells Us* (New York: College Board, 2008).

[35]Annie Hsiao, "Congressman Ryan's Budget Proposal on Pell Grants: Effectiveness over Popularity," *Daily Caller*, April 12, 2011, http://dailycaller .com/2011/04/12/congressman-ryans-budget-proposal-on-pell-grants -effectiveness-over-popularity.

[36]Julie Margetta Morgan, "Address the Root Causes of Pell Grant Costs Before Cutting It," *Campus Progress*, July 25, 2011, www.campusprogress.org/ articles/address_the_root_causes_of_pell_grant_costs_before_cutting_it.

[37]Mark Kantrowitz, "Preserving the Pell Grant: Alternatives to Cutting Year-Round Pell or the Maximum Grant," *FinAid*, April 4, 2011, www.finaid.org/ educators/20110329preservingpell.pdf.

[38]Alexander Bolton, "Conservatives Angry Over Pell Grant Funding in Boehner Debt Bill," *Hill News Alerts*, July 28, 2011.

[39]Hsiao, "Congressman Ryan's Budget Proposal on Pell Grants."

[40]Joe Klein, "Time to Ax Public Programs That Don't Yield Results," *Time*, July 7, 2011, www.time.com/time/nation/article/0,8599,2081778,00.html #ixzz1aVPgcWQ8; and "Head Start Impact Study," U.S. Department of Health and Human Services, 2010, www.acf.hhs.gov/programs/opre/hs/ impact_study/reports/impact_study/hs_impact_study_final.pdf.

[41]"Long-Term Benefits," HighScope Educational Research Foundation, n.d., www.highscope.org/Content.asp?ContentId=260; "Benefits of Head Start (HS) and Early Head Start (EHS) Programs," National Head Start Association Research and Evaluation Department, n. d., www.nhsa.org/ files/static_page_files/081FD64E-1D09-3519-ADC7E878DDB5CEC9/ REDFactSheets1.pdf; Sherri Oden, Lawrence Schweinhart, and David Weikart, *Into Adulthood: A Study of the Effects of Head Start* (Ypsilanti, Mich.: High/Scope Press, 2000); David Deming, "Early Childhood Intervention and Life-Cycle Skill Development: Evidence From Head Start," *American Economic Journal: Applied Economics* 1, no. 3 (2009): 111-34; and Chloe Gibbs, Jens Ludwig, and Douglas Miller, "Does Head Start Do Any Lasting Good?," National Bureau of Economic Research Working

Paper No. 17452, September 2011, www.nber.org/papers/w17452.pdf.

[42]W. Steven Barnett and Jason Hustedt, "Head Start's Lasting Benefits." *Infants and Young Children* 18, no. 1 (2005): 16-24.

[43]Jason DeParle, Robert Gebeloff, and Sabrina Tavernise, "Bleak Portrait of Poverty Is Off the Mark, Experts Say," *New York Times*, November 3, 2011, p. A1,www.nytimes.com/2011/11/04/us/experts-say-bleak-account-of-poverty -missed-the-mark.html?pagewanted=1&ref=sabrinatavernise.

[44]"American Public Vastly Overestimates Amount of U.S. Foreign Aid," *World Public Opinion.org*, November 29, 2010, accessed October 13, 2011, www .worldpublicopinion.org/pipa/articles/brunitedstatescanadara/670.php.

[45]"Policy Basics: Where Do Our Tax Dollars Go?," CBPP, April 15, 2011, www.cbpp.org/cms/index.cfm?fa=view&id=1258.

[46]Curt Tarnoff and Marian Leonardo Lawson, "Foreign Aid," CRS R40213, February 10, 2011; see summary of the paper and p. 8.

[47]BFW, "2012 Hunger Report," intro.

[48]Tarnoff and Lawson, "Foreign Aid," p. 13.

[49]"PEPFAR Funding," U.S. State Department, June 2011, www.pepfar.gov/ press/80064.htm; accessed September 23, 2011.

[50]See, for example, the discussion in BFW, "2012 Hunger Report," chap. 4.

[51]Molly Lester, "International Affairs Budget Update, 7-27-11," U.S. Global Leadership Coalition, July 27, 2011, www.usglc.org/2011/07/27/interna tional-affairs-budget-update-7-27-11. The Senate committee retained a great deal more of the President's request; see "International Affairs Budget Update, 9-22-11," U.S. Global Leadership Coalition, September 22, 2011, www.usglc.org/2011/09/22/international-affairs-budgetupdate-9-22-11.

[52]Michael Gerson, "The GOP's Door of No Return." *Washington Post*, February 15, 2011.

[53]Robert McIntyre et al., "Corporate Taxpayers & Corporate Tax Dodgers: 2008-10," Citizens for Tax Justice and the Institute of Taxation and Economic Policy, November 2011, www.ctj.org/corporatetaxdodgers/Corpora teTaxDodgersReport.pdf.

[54]The Ryan budget cuts $127 billion from SNAP over the next ten years; estimates for WIC and foreign food assistance are based on 2010 expenditures of $6.7 and $2 billion, respectively.

[55]For an excellent overview of the farm bill, see Jim Monke and Renée Johnson, "Actual Farm Bill Spending," CRS R41195, April 20, 2010.

[56]BFW, "2012 Hunger Report," chap. 1.

[57]See the speech in the House by Republican Congressman Frank Wolf on October 4, 2011, denouncing Norquist; "Wolf: Norquist's Relationships Should Give People Pause," Congressman Frank Wolf, October 4, 2011, http://wolf

.house.gov/index.cfm?sectionid=34&sectiontree=6,34&itemid=1805.

[58]BFW, "2012 Hunger Report," chap. 1.

[59]Avi Feller and Chuck Maw, "Tax Rate For Richest 400 Plummeted in Recent Decades, Even as their Pre-Tax Incomes Skyrocketed," CBPP, February 23, 2010.

[60]Molly F. Sherlock, "Reducing the Budget Deficit," CRS R41641, April 26, 2011, p. 8.

[61]Warren E. Buffett, "Stop Coddling the Super-rich," *New York Times*, August 14, 2011.

[62]Sherlock, "Reducing the Budget Deficit," p. 3.

[63]Chuck Colson, "Ideology and the Budget Deal," *Breakpoint*, August 3, 2011.

[64]"Budget, Taxes, Economic Policy," PollingReport.com, www.pollingreport.com/budget.htm.

[65]Buffett, "Stop Coddling the Super-rich." The figure of 36% is a bit puzzling since the highest income tax bracket is 35%. But Buffett's article says the average rate for the rest in his office was 36%.

[66]Robert J. Samuelson, "The Real Tax Avoidance Scandal Centers on Dividends and Capital Gains," *Washington Post*, April 3, 2011.

[67]Nelson D. Schwartz and Louise Story, "Pay of Hedge Fund Managers Roared Back Last Year," *New York Times*, March 31, 2010, www.nytimes.com/2010/04/01/business/01hedge.html, accessed October 31, 2011.

[68]Feller and Marr, "Tax Rate," CBPP, February 23, 2011, p. 2.

[69]Buffett, "Stop Coddling the Super-rich."

[70]Simpson-Bowles, p. 31.

[71]Ibid., p. 28. Simpson and Bowles do make other adjustments. But their own figure 8 shows that taxes increase for the second lowest quintile by a higher percentage than for any other quintile.

[72]Jeffrey Miron, "Why Warren Buffett Is Wrong," *CNN Opinion*, August 16, 2011, http://articles.cnn.com/2011-08-16/opinion/miron.buffett.wrong_1_income-tax-code-crony-capitalism?_s=PM:OPINION.

[73]See chart in *New York Times*, April 16, 2011, p. A17.

[74]For example, Martin Feldstein, President Reagan's chairman of the Council of Economic Advisors, and Len Burman, deputy assistant secretary of the Treasury under President Clinton.

[75]Sherlock, "Reducing the Budget Deficit," p. 12.

[76]Ibid.

[77]Donna Cooper, "Infographic: Tax Breaks vs. Budget Cuts," Center For American Progress, February 22, 2011, www.americanprogress.org/issues/2011/02/tax_breaks_infographic.html.

[78]Simpson-Bowles, p. 30, specifically recommends keeping these tax credits.

[79]There might however be other ways (e.g., a refundable tax credit) to accomplish the same goal; see "Alms from the Working Class," *Portfolio.com*, www.portfolio.com/graphics/2008/02/Alms-From-the-Working-Class.

[80]Simpson-Bowles, pp. 29-30.

[81]This rate has been temporarily lowered to strengthen the economy.

[82]Sherlock, "Reducing the Budget Deficit," p. 18.

[83]Bill Gates Sr., quoted in Chuck Collins and Mary Wright, *The Moral Measure of the Economy* (Maryknoll, N.Y.: Orbis, 2007), p. 103.

[84]Warren E. Buffett, quoted in David Cay Johnston, "Dozens of Rich Americans Join in Fight to Retain the Estate Tax," *New York Times*, February 14, 2001.

[85]See National Research Council, *Advancing the Science of Climate Change* (Washington, D.C.: National Academies Press, 2010): http://books.nap.edu/openbook.php?record_id=12782&page=R1#; and International Panel on Climate Change, Fourth Assessment Report (AR4), Working Group One (WG1), Summary for Policymakers (SPM). IPCC reports can be found at their website, www.ipcc.ch. In its last year in office the Bush Administration issued a major report on climate change that affirmed these findings of the IPCC. See "Scientific Assessment of the Effects of Global Change on the United States," National Science and Technology Council, May 2008, www.whitehouse.gov/files/documents/ostp/NSTC%20Reports/Scientific%20Assessment%20FULL%20Report.pdf (esp. pp. 1-7). Also Katharine Hayhoe and Andrew Farley, *A Climate for Change: Global Warming Facts for Faith-based Decisions* (New York: FaithWorks, 2009).

[86]The amount depends largely on the amount of the tax per ton of emissions. See Sherlock, "Reducing the Budget Deficit," p. 20.

[87]Paul Krugman, "Things to Tax," *New York Times*, November 28, 2011, p. A21.

[88]For example, there is considerable support for changing the corporate income tax. Lowering the rate (to make it more nearly comparable to other industrialized nations) is probably a good idea if at the same time we end many tax expenditures in the tax so that at least there is no loss of federal revenue. See ibid., pp. 15-18.

[89]Ryan, "Path to Prosperity," p. 51. For another example of this argument see Amity Shlaes, "Want to Create Jobs? First Cut Capital-Gains Taxes," *Bloomberg*, October 26, 2011, www.bloomberg.com/news/2011-10-26/want-to-create-jobs-first-cut-capital-gains-taxes-amity-shlaes.html.

[90]Harry Holzer and Edward Montgomery, "Which Tax Cuts Actually Create Jobs?" *Politico*, December 6, 2010, www.politico.com/news/stories/1210/46007.html#ixzzlcVpEz5x9. See also John Irons and Josh Bivens, "A Feeble

Recovery: The Fundamental Economic Weaknesses of the 2001-07 Expansion," Economic Policy Institute, December 9, 2008.

[91]Curtis Dubay, "Setting the Tax Record Straight: Clinton Hikes Slowed Growth, Bush Cuts Promoted Recovery," The Heritage Foundation, September 6, 2011, www.heritage.org/Research/Reports/2011/09/Settingthe-Tax-Record-Straight-Clinton-Hikes-Slowed-Growth-Bush-Cuts-Promoted-Recovery; "Bush On Jobs: The Worst Track Record On Record," *Wall Street Journal*, January 9, 2009, http://blogs.wsj.com/economics/2009/01/09/bush-on-jobs-the-worst-track-record-on-record; and Paul Waldman, "Show Me the Numbers," August 18, 2011, *American Prospect*, http://prospect.org/article/show-me-the-numbers.

[92]D. Wilson and William Beach, "The Economic Impact of President Bush's Tax Relief Plan," The Heritage Foundation, April 27, 2001, www.heritage.org/research/reports/2001/04/the-economic-impact-of-president-bushs-tax-relief-plan.

[93]Heather Boushey and Adam Hersh, "Ryan's Unbelievable Path to Prosperity," Center for American Progress, April 6, 2011, www.americanprogress.org/issues/2011/04/ryan_heritage.html. The Heritage Foundation uses the IHS Global Insight model.

[94]Dubay, "Setting the Tax Record Straight."

[95]"The Bush Tax Cuts Disproportionately Benefitted the Wealthy," Economic Policy Institute, June 4, 2011, www.epi.org/publication/the_bush_tax_cuts_disproportionately_benefitted_the_wealthy.

[96]"Household Income Up Slightly in 2007, But Down Since 2000," U.S. Congress Joint Economic Committee, August 26, 2008, http://jec.senate.gov/public/?a=Files.Serve&File_id=716285e1-5e2a-4587-a83f-72b9ead741d5.

[97]Tina Dupuy, "The Man Behind Paul Ryan's Budget Plan Got the Tax Cuts Wrong, Too," *The Atlantic*, April 15, 2011, www.theatlantic.com/politics/archive/2011/04/the-man-behind-paul-ryans-budget-plan-got-the-tax-cuts-wrong-too/237360.

[98]For example, "The Economic Effects of the Ryan Plan: Assuming the Answer?" *Macroeconomic Advisers* (blog), April 14, 2011, http://macroadvisers.blogspot.com/2011/04/economic-effects-of-ryan-plan-assuming.html; Menzie Chinn, "More on the Characteristics of the Heritage Foundation CDA Analysis of the Ryan Plan," *Econbrowser*, April 14, 2011, www.econbrowser.com/archives/2011/04/more_on_the_cha_1.html.

[99]William Beach et al., "Economic Analysis of the House Budget Resolution," The Heritage Foundation, April 5, 2011, www.heritage.org/Research/Reports/2011/04/Economic-Analysis-of-the-House-Budget-Resolution.

[100]"Average Federal Tax Rates for All Households, by Comprehensive

Household Income Quintile, 1979-2007," CBO, June 2010, www.cbo
.gov/publications/collections/tax/2010/average_rates.pdf; "Taxes on the
Wealthy Have Gone Down Dramatically," Economic Policy Institute, April
14, 2011, www.epi.org/publication/taxes_on_the_wealthy_have_gone_down
_dramatically.

[101]Mark Drajem and Catherine Dodge, "Obama Wrote 5% Fewer Rules Than
Bush While Costing Business," Bloomberg, October 25, 2011, www
.bloomberg.com/news/2011-10-25/obama-wrote-5-fewer-rules-than-bush
-while-costing-business.html.

[102]For example, Alan Beattie, "IMF Urges Financial Regulation Co-
ordination," Financial Times, March 6, 2009, www.ft.com/cms/s/0/852bf056
-09e2-11de-add8-0000779fd2ac.html#axzz1cYjOmUPJ.

[103]Matt Krantz and Barbara Hansen, "CEO Pay Soars While Workers' Pay
Stalls," USA Today, April 4, 2011, www.usatoday.com/money/companies/
management/story/CEO-pay-2010/45634384/1; Sarah Anderson et al.,
"CEO Pay and the Great Recession," Institute for Policy Studies, September 1, 2010, www.ips-dc.org/files/2433/EE-2010-web.pdf.

[104]"Distribution of Tax Units with Small Business Income, 2007," Tax Policy
Center, April 27, 2007, www.taxpolicycenter.org/numbers/displayatab.cf
m?DocID=1534&topic2ID=150&topic3ID=156&DocTypeID=.

[105]Mark Zandi, "At Last, the U.S. Begins a Serious Fiscal Debate," Moody's
Analytics, April 14, 2011, www.economy.com/dismal/article_free.asp?cid=
198972&src=msnbc.

[106]"Policies for Increasing Economic Growth and Employment in 2010 and
2011," CBO, January 2010, www.cbo.gov/ftpdocs/108xx/doc10803/01-14-
Employment.pdf.

[107]Figure displayed in Concurrent Resolution on the Budget—Fiscal Year 2012,
Report of the Committee on the Budget, House of Representatives, "The
Path to Prosperity: Restoring America's Promise," April 5, 2011, p. 12.

[108]Paul N. Van de Water and Arloc Sherman, "Social Security," CBPP, August
11, 2010.

[109]"Policy Basics," CBPP, August 13, 2010, p. 1.

[110]See n. 125 in this chapter for details.

[111]CBPP, "Policy Basics," p. 5.

[112]Ibid., p. 3.

[113]Ibid., p. 5.

[114]Domenici-Rivlin, p. 71.

[115]Ibid.

[116]CBPP, "Policy Basics," p. 6.

[117]Using the old formula of the Census Bureau, the poverty level for children

in 2010 was 22% and only 9% for seniors. But the new, more accurate formula indicates that the poverty rate for children is 18.2% and that for seniors is 15.9%. Unfortunately, the new poverty formula exaggerates the poverty of seniors because it does not count income from savings, stock market, etc. See Sabrina Tavernise and Robert Gebeloff, "New Way to Tally Poor," *New York Times*, November 8, 2011, p. A15, and Tami Luhby, "Poverty Rate Rises Under Alternate Census Measure," *CNN Money*, November 7, 2011, http://money.cnn.com/2011/11/07/news/economy/poverty_rate/index.htm.

[118]Fareed Zakaria, "The Hard Truth About Going 'Soft,'" *Time*, October 17, 2011, p. 26.

[119]Individuals with a combined income of $25,000-$34,000 ($32,000-$44,000 for couples) pay income tax on up to 50% of their benefits. Individuals with combined income over $34,000 (over $44,000 for couples) pay tax on up to 85%.

[120]Robert J. Samuelson, "Why Social Security Is Welfare," *Washington Post*, March 7, 2011.

[121]Andrew Fieldhouse and Isaac Shapiro, "The Facts Support Raising Revenues from Highest-Income Households," Economic Policy Institute, August 5, 2011, www.epi.org/publication/the_facts_support_raising_rev enues_from_the_highest-income_households.

[122]Simpson-Bowles, p. 51.

[123]Ibid., p. 50

[124]See Domenici-Rivlin, p. 75, and Simpson-Bowles, pp. 51-52, both of whom recommend this change.

[125]Currently, retirees receive 90% of the first $749 of the worker's average monthly earnings; 32% of the average monthly earnings between $749 and $4,517 and 15% above that (Domenici-Rivlin, p. 73). Domenici-Rivlin recommend reducing the top bracket from 15% to 10% over thirty years (p. 76). We also need some upper limit for social security benefits.

[126]Domenici-Rivlin suggests that from ages 81 to 85, we should increase their benefits by 1% per year (p. 80).

[127]See for example Damian Paletta, "Disability-Claim Judge Has Trouble Saying 'No,'" *Wall Street Journal*, May 19, 2011, http://online.wsj.com/article/SB10001424052748704681904576319163605918524.html. On the other hand, there are long backlogs in hearing social security disability cases. That too should be corrected.

[128]See, for example, Joe Klein, "Where the Tea Party Runs Strong," *Time*, October 3, 2011, p. 23.

[129]CBPP, "Policy Basics," p. 3.

[130]Gary Bauer, "Save Social Security, Save Our Families," *New York Times*, January 23, 1997, op-ed page.

[131]Simpson-Bowles, pp. 36, 41.

[132]For a good overview, see Patricia A. Davis, "Medicare Primer," CRS RL40425, July 1, 2010.

[133]See Elicia J. Herz, "Medicaid: A Primer," CRS RL33202, January 11, 2011.

[134]Gina Kolata, "First Study of Its Kind Shows Benefits of Providing Medical Insurance to Poor," *New York Times*, July 7, 2011.

[135]Patricia A. Davis, "Medicare Program Changes in H.R. 3962," CRS R40898, November 9, 2009, p. 2.

[136]Jennifer O'Sullivan, "Medicare: A Primer," CRS RL33712, August 1, 2008, p. 32.

[137]Ibid.

[138]Paul N. Van de Water, "Medicare Is Not 'Bankrupt,'" CBPP, July 12, 2011, p. 2.

[139]"Projected Spending on Health Care as a Percentage of Gross Domestic Product," CBO, www.cbo.gov/ftpdocs/87xx/doc8758/MainText.3.1.shtml #1068878.

[140]"Health Care Spending in the United States and Selected OECD Countries," Kaiser Family Foundation, April 2011, www.kff.org/insurance/snapshot/OECD042111.cfm.

[141]Nelson D. Schwartz, "Swiss Model," *New York Times*, October 1, 2009, pp. A1, A3.

[142]Domenici-Rivlin, p. 45; see also Ezekiel J. Emanuel and Jeffrey B. Liebman, "Cut Medicare, Help Patients," *New York Times*, August 23, 2011, p. A21.

[143]BFW, "2012 Hunger Report," chap. 1.

[144]Ibid., chap. 2.

[145]This figure has remained fairly constant for decades. Ezekiel J. Emanuel and Linda L. Emanuel, "The Economics of Dying—The Illusion of Cost Savings at the End of Life," *New England Journal of Medicine*, February 24, 1994, 540; "Debate Surrounds End-of-Life Health Care Costs," *USA Today*, October 18, 2006.

[146]Gina Kolata, "Surgery Rate Late in Life Surprises Researchers," *New York Times*, October 6, 2011, p. A19.

[147]Ibid.

[148]Emanuel and Emanuel, "Economics of Dying," p. 540.

[149]See, for example, my *Completely Pro Life: Building a Consistent Stance* (Downers Grove, Ill.: InterVarsity Press, 1987).

[150]Apparently, we do not have careful accurate studies of the amount of these

costs. Emanuel and Emanuel rather doubt that huge savings are possible with more widespread use of living wills, hospice care, etc. But their article "Economics of Dying" is more than fifteen years old.

[151]Ezekiel J. Emanuel and Jeffrey B. Liebman, "Cut Medicare," *New York Times*, August 23, 2011, p. A21.

[152]Simpson-Bowles, pp. 36-43; Domenici-Rivlin, pp. 44-69.

[153]Simpson-Bowles, pp. 37-38.

[154]Ibid., p. 38.

[155]Domenici-Rivlin, p. 94.

[156]Ibid., p. 19.

[157]Brian Riedl, "50 Examples of Government Waste," The Heritage Foundation, October 6, 2009, www.heritage.org/Research/Reports/2009/10/50-Examples-of-Government-Waste.

[158]Gordon Adams and Matthew Leatherman, "A Leaner and Meaner Defense," *Foreign Affairs*, January-February 2011, pp. 139-52.

[159]Ibid., p. 140.

[160]Ibid.

[161]Ibid., p. 152.

[162]Steven Greenhut, "Howard Ahmanson Becomes a Democrat Seriously," *Orange County Register*, March 23, 2009.

Chapter 6: We Can Do It

[1]For this section on tax loopholes, see Ron Nixon and Eric Lichtblau, "In Debt Talks, All Tax Breaks Are Not Alike," *New York Times*, October 3, 2011, pp. A1, A3.

[2]BFW, *Bread*, July-August 2011, p. 1.

Index

DATE DUE

 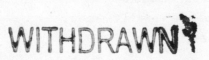